# POPE ALEXANDER III
# AND THE COUNCIL OF TOURS

*Published under the auspices of the*

## CENTER FOR MEDIEVAL AND RENAISSANCE STUDIES

*University of California, Los Angeles*

ROBERT SOMERVILLE

# Pope Alexander III
# and the Council of Tours
# (1163)

## A Study of Ecclesiastical Politics
## and Institutions in the Twelfth Century

UNIVERSITY OF CALIFORNIA PRESS
Berkeley, Los Angeles, London

The emblem of the Center for Medieval and Renaissance Studies reproduces the imperial eagle of the
gold *augustalis* struck after 1231 by Emperor Frederick II; Elvira and Vladimir Clain-Stefanelli, *The
Beauty and Lore of Coins, Currency and Medals*
(Croton-on-Hudson, 1974), fig, 130 and p. 106.

University of California Press
Berkeley and Los Angeles, California

University of California Press, Ltd.
London, England

ISBN: 0-520-03184-9
Library of Congress Catalog Card Number: 75-46043
Copyright © 1977 by The Regents of the University of California

Printed in the United States of America

1 2 3 4 5 6 7 8 9 0

to
Paul Oskar Kristeller

# Contents

# Preface

Raymonde Foreville's observation of a decade ago that "the medieval councils scarcely have been studied"[1] applies to no group of synods more readily than the papal assemblies of the eleventh and twelfth centuries. To a great extent, this lacuna results from the state of the printed documentation. Conciliar historians are confronted by a series of formidable volumes of source material assembled prior to 1800, of which Mansi, *Amplissima collectio,* is the latest and best known (although not the most carefully prepared).[2] At first glance, these tomes can appear well ordered and exhaustive, but investigation reveals how confusing and often confused the presentations are. To rely on such collections can be hazardous, yet Hefele-Leclercq's narrative *Histoire des conciles* from early in this century, which leans heavily and often uncritically on Mansi and his predecessors, has become a standard reference tool in ecclesiastical history. The so-called ecumenical councils of the twelfth century—the Lateran assemblies of 1123, 1139, and 1179— recently have been studied together in one volume by Mlle. Foreville;[3] but apart from Pope Urban II's convocation at Clermont in 1095, no papal synod from this period has received modern monographic attention.[4]

   The present study and its predecessor on Clermont are historiographic innovations, although of different sorts. The latter is more specialized, and is occupied only with recovering the conciliar decrees. Their transmission is muddled, hence the synod's position within the reforming movement of the eleventh and twelfth centuries can be distorted or even neglected. Moreover, since Pope Urban II inaugurated the First Crusade at Clermont, the assembly easily can be regarded as the "crusade council," and overlooked as an important element in a series of papal gatherings devoted to reform. These observations are not new;[5] but a volume concerned with retrieving the decrees will emphasize the proper historical perspective for the event. Such a work also is valuable as a methodological example for other synods with jumbled canonical traditions from the so-called Gregorian and post-Gregorian decades.

The 1163 council at Tours met amidst the most protracted conflict between a pope and a secular ruler in medieval history, the eighteen-year struggle between Alexander III and Frederick Barbarossa. The gathering duly receives a paragraph or so in surveys of that dispute,[6] and it usually is included—and properly so—in lists of the important sources for twelfth- and thirteenth-century canon law.[7] But the meeting has been accorded no integrated study of all its political and legislative facets, nor have all of the sources, even all of those available in print, ever been utilized together.

Although the transmission of the canons from Tours is not without problems, these texts do not require the special attention demanded by those from Clermont. A critical edition is desirable, but a study of the council need not be postponed for lack of it.[8] The uncertainties raised by the decrees can be treated within a general investigation. The present work strives, therefore, to offer in one volume a historical account of the synod at Tours which is as complete as possible. That means uncovering the conciliar events as well as pondering their relation to the great issues of the time, especially Alexander's struggle with Frederick. The aim is to reconstruct, as the sources permit, what happened at a council of acknowledged import, and at the same time to examine the interdependence of those events with the historical climate in which the gathering convened. Such reciprocity often has become hazy, but synods do not assemble in a vacuum. Their histories gain greater fascination in proportion to how successfully the events *in concilio* can be linked to movements and pressures from society at large. As John Gilchrist remarked in his work on the medieval Church and economic activity, a synod ought to be investigated "as a unity, that is the events leading up to, through and after the council, to the point where the decrees have become part of the tradition of canon law."[9]

Alexander presided at only three councils during a pontificate of more than two decades. The great assembly at the Lateran in 1179 merits a separate study, in view of its extensive legislation and the changing political climate. The other two synods met one year apart—at Montpellier in May 1162, and at Tours in May 1163. The former is very poorly documented, and what little is known will be incorporated here. The gathering at Tours has fared better, including the fortunate survival of a detailed attendance catalogue; but the sources are episodic, and hence unsuited for recounting day-by-day activities. The following format has been adopted. The opening chapter surveys portions of Alexander's early years as pope, and describes the need and the preparation for the assembly in 1163. The middle chapters (2–6) examine topics related to conciliar operations and decisions. The final section is an epilogue, assessing in particular the council's political import.

An effort has been made to compress and abbreviate the notes. All titles shortened there are listed in the Bibliography. Latin texts are, for the most part, not reproduced but only cited, and translations are the author's unless indicated. Personal names generally are Anglicized.

The author is indebted to several colleagues, friends, and institutions. Professors J. M. W. Bean, John H. Mundy, Edward M. Peters, Eugene F. Rice, Jr., and especially Robert L. Benson and Giles Constable, read versions of this study, and offered valuable criticisms and advice. Professor Stephan Kuttner, the staff of the Institute of Medieval Canon Law, and the Law School of the University of California, Berkeley, provided stimulating hospitality during the period when this work was achieving final form, and Professor Kuttner's matchless knowledge of medieval legal and ecclesiastical history provided insights into various problems relating to the Council of Tours. Careful preparation of the typescript for the printer by Dr. Carol D. Lanham, Editorial Coordinator at the Center for Medieval and Renaissance Studies, University of California, Los Angeles, saved the author from both blunders and infelicitous phrases. Sections of this book were researched and written while the author was supported by a John Simon Guggenheim Memorial Fellowship and a Chamberlain Fellowship from Columbia University. The Dunning Fund of the History Department at Columbia helped to defray typing expenses. Finally, the author is grateful to Professor Robin Ann Aronstam, Charles Caritiain, Dr. John M. George, and Dr. Thomas G. Waldman.

*Columbia University*
*May 1977*

# 1

## Introduction

### BACKGROUND

Since the days are evil and much must be tolerated in view of the quality of the times, we request, warn, advise, and urge you to be cautious, foreseeing, and circumspect in all matters both personal and ecclesiastical. Do not act hastily or rashly but, as far as is possible saving the freedom of the Church and the esteem of your office, opportunely and with dignity, in order to regain the favor and goodwill of the illustrious English king. . . . Then the Lord will grant better times, and both you and we can pursue this matter more freely.[1]

So in 1165 Pope Alexander III wrote to Thomas Becket, then in exile from Canterbury at Pontigny. In counseling the archbishop to be patient in the face of turmoil, Alexander must have reflected on his own recent problems. The political tensions gathering around the papacy in the 1150s exploded after the death of Hadrian IV in 1159.[2] Separate elections by different groups of cardinals had resulted in two pontiffs—Alexander and Victor IV—representing the "papal" and "imperial" sides in the ensuing conflict.[3] For the second time in less than three decades the Roman Church was torn by a schism. When he wrote to Thomas in 1165, Alexander had not seen Rome for four years, nor Italy itself for more than three. He had been hounded by the emperor Frederick Barbarossa and imperial supporters until his presence south of the Alps became impossible. Following the example of Pope Innocent II thirty years earlier,[4] he fled to France, sailing at Eastertide in 1162 from the vicinity of Genoa toward Montpellier. His arrival there was greeted by a throng so enthusiastic and large that "whoever with great effort could touch the tip of his cloak, thought himself fortunate."[5] Like Thomas at Pontigny, however, Alexander was a refugee.[6]

1

His objectives in France were the same as Innocent's had been. He needed material support, such as suitable residences, as well as public opinion favorable to him and to his cause. On 30 April 1162, Alexander wrote to the French queen Adele, "In the most holy Roman Church the glorious memory of your ancestors, who . . . always were devoted and fervent in allegiance to blessed Peter, remains vivid. . . ."[7] The pope urged Adele to imitate such conduct, and to strive especially to encourage her husband King Louis VII in appropriate Petrine devotion. A similarly worded appeal had been sent from Italy during the previous year directly to the king.[8] Such language no doubt was meant to recall Louis VI and Innocent II, despite the fact that Louis had been less decisive for Innocent's triumph than churchmen such as St. Bernard of Clairvaux.[9]

The political and ecclesiastical issues in 1162 were complicated. Both England and France had declared formally for Alexander, but King Louis's position was awkward. Across his eastern border was the Empire, and the prime supporters of Victor IV. Frederick Barbarossa was not beyond rattling sabres at a weaker neighbor to achieve a purpose. In a letter to Bishop Hugh of Soissons, who served as royal chancellor, he expressed his displeasure at Alexander's presence in France:

We have actually heard that Roland, formerly (papal) chancellor, who, because of those loyal to us, does not have and cannot find a place in Rome to lay his head, has entered France by sea with his pseudo-supporters. . . . Imploring you, therefore, with deep and abundant affection, we warn that you should in no way receive the aforesaid schismatic, a hideous enemy of us and of our entire empire, nor should you permit him to be received by anyone. In good faith advise the French king to receive neither him nor any of his pseudo-cardinals nor ambassadors. For on that account great enmity, which we could not easily suppress or calm, would arise between our empire and your kingdom.[10]

Of comparable difficulty for King Louis was that he could not trust his western neighbor either. Henry Plantagenet was the French monarch's vassal, but his possessions, stretching from Gascony to Scotland, dwarfed the Capetian domain. In late July 1160 the two rulers had met at Beauvais.[11] With their clergy and imperial observers, they listened to arguments from envoys of the papal competitors. The Alexandrians prevailed, but not without concessions in Henry's favor which clouded relations between the kings for the next two years.[12]

Yet Louis did not desert Alexander. He was bound to him by the preference of a majority of his churchmen, as well as by the considerable influence which Henry could exert over French policy. As Mary Cheney has written, "Louis could not risk declaring for one pope and seeing his rival take all western France into the other obedience."[13] But between the summer of

1160 and the fall of 1162 he was cool toward Alexander, and in frequent contact with the opposition. The pope had good reason to implore Queen Adele's intercession with her husband.

Whatever their hopes, those in Victor's camp did not seriously believe that Louis would embrace their candidate.[14] By late summer of 1162, after particularly embarrassing treatment from the Germans, the French king was willing to meet with Alexander and Henry.[15] Writing to Louis from Déols on September 17, the pope employed considerable diplomatic skill to repair his alliance and to lay the foundation for a tripartite conference.[16] He sympathized about the "iniquity and cunning of Frederick and his advisers," and reported that Henry, urged to display the respect and support due an overlord, had dispatched envoys to Louis, through whom he would offer "himself, his land, and all the forces at his disposal for the honor, security, and exaltation of your kingdom." Hardly indifferent, the pope exhorted the Capetian ruler to receive this delegation kindly and with gratitude. Perhaps to ease the memory of his legates' actions at Beauvais, Alexander terminated the letter by professing his constant solicitude for French concerns.

The meeting between the pontiff and the two rulers took place *super Ligerim apud Cociacum:* the sole account is provided by Robert of Torigny, abbot of Mont St.-Michel from 1154 to 1186, and there seems to be no reason to disregard it.[17] Apart from a location on the Loire, however, historians have been inconsistent about the identity of this place. It has been designated as Choisi, Chouzé, Chouzy, and Coucy.[18] Accepting Robert's account to mean what it says, Choisi and Coucy can be dismissed, since there appear to be no such localities in the Loire Valley.[19] Chouzé-sur-Loire (Indre-et-Loire), is on the north bank of the river, about seven kilometers from Bourgueil. A priory of Bourgueil, Le Plessis-aux-Moines, existed there from the eleventh century,[20] and Robert could have been indicating Chouzé. But there is another prospect which is at least equally likely.

In the nineteenth century, there still existed southwest of Blois an "ancienne petite ville située à dix kilomètres, sur la rive gauche [north] de la Loire," named Chouzy.[21] This village would have been adjacent to the present town of Chouzy-sur-Cisse. One nineteenth-century description of the latter settlement noted that it reached both the Loire and the Cisse;[22] and the extent to which Chouzy-sur-Loire survives today as an entity distinct from Chouzy-sur-Cisse is undetermined.[23] A priory of Marmoutier, dedicated to St. Martin, was established at Chouzy-sur-Loire in the eleventh century, and in 1276 the nunnery of La Guiche was founded in the same area.[24]

A cautious preference can be expressed for this spot as the site of the royal-papal meeting in the autumn of 1162.[25] The priory of St. Martin could have provided those comforts necessary for such a colloquy, and the location was almost exactly on the boundary between Capetian and Angevin territory. No doubt similar amenities would have been available at Chouzé-sur-Loire, but a meeting at Chouzé between Louis and Henry would have required the French king to journey deep into Touraine, which was in Henry's domain. That might have presented various difficulties for both monarchs.

Since Robert is the unique source, the episode may not have been meant to generate publicity. Its absence from Cardinal Boso's *Vita* of Alexander III strengthens this supposition, for although Boso's work is not without problems and inaccuracies,[26] he was at that time with the pope.[27] The *Vita* offers instead an account of Henry II meeting with Alexander at Déols.[28] This must have happened on or soon after September 18, since in his letter to Louis on the 17th, the pope was expecting Henry the following day.[29] The two leaders reportedly conferred for three days; and Alexander remained in Déols at least until September 24.[30] Assuming that Henry arrived on the 18th, and that the conference did last three days, the monarch and the pontiff probably made their way northward separately to encounter Louis. This carefully arranged rendezvous would have occurred, in all likelihood, during the first week of October,[31] at what must have been a judiciously chosen spot.

R. W. Southern has observed that papal primacy in the Middle Ages "would never have been effective if lay rulers had not found that, even if it offered them nothing, it took almost nothing from them."[32] Primacy was not the issue *apud Cociacum,* yet both Henry and Louis must have realized that there was minimal risk in joining Alexander there. The pope needed them badly, and was in no position to create difficulties. Henry had little to fear from Frederick Barbarossa, and his promise of military support would calm Louis. A tent was prepared for the three dignitaries. The two kings, one on each side of Alexander's horse, performed the honorific bridle ceremony (*officium stratoris*) for the pope—the same ritual which in the previous decade had provoked an incident between Hadrian IV and the impetuous Barbarossa.[33]

This meeting near Tours happened only weeks after a Victorine council. Alexander's opponents had gathered in early September in the vicinity of St.-Jean-de-Losne, but certainly in imperial Burgundy, following the collapse of Frederick and Louis's venture to convene a synod including both popes to resolve the schism.[34] In the presence of the emperor, King Waldemar of Denmark, and the German clergy, Alexander and his adherents were condemned. Rainald of Dassel, the imperial chancellor and archbishop of Cologne, is reported to have asked how the rulers of England and France would view meddling by the emperor in an episcopal dispute in their realms.

Analogously, Rainald contended, these "provincial kings" should not inter-
fere in the ecclesiastical affairs of Rome.[35]

This was not the first council against Alexander. Similar assemblies had
met at Pavia (February 1160) and Lodi (June 1161); and in early November
1162, subsequent to the Burgundian synod, Victor convoked German and
Italian clerics at Trier, where the Alexandrians again were castigated.[36] Between the dual election in 1159 and the end of 1162 no fewer than five papal
councils are recorded. Four were Victorine, including the gathering arranged
by Frederick at Pavia, ostensibly to negotiate an impartial end to the
schism,[37] and one was Alexandrian, at Montpellier in 1162.[38] This forms a
striking contrast with the twenty-year period between the 1139 Lateran
Council and the death of Hadrian IV in 1159, when only two papal councils can be found, both under Eugene III in 1148 (Reims and Cremona).[39]

The Alexandrian-Victorine revival of synodal activity finds a parallel in
the years before 1139. Following Calixtus II's assembly at the Lateran in
1123, no important papal councils appear until 1130.[40] Lateran I marked an
end to the secular-ecclesiastical struggles of the previous decades; and
whether or not "an age of peaceful growth" truly had been initiated,[41] the
newly defined concord between *regnum* and *sacerdotium* undoubtedly would
help to account for the subdued level of conciliar operations under Honorius
II. But less than a decade after the compromise on investiture with the
emperor Henry V, a dual election following Honorius's death in 1130 engendered a schism in the Roman Church.[42]

Several well-documented synods were convened as a result, especially by
the sometime fugitive Innocent II during the first half of the decade.[43] The
struggle ended in Innocent's favor with the great assembly at the Lateran in
1139. But subsequent to that event, aside from Eugene III's gatherings in
1148 papal conciliar life seems to have been dormant for more than twenty
years.[44] It has been implied that the troubles concomitant with Arnold of
Brescia's appearance at Rome hindered Eugene and Hadrian IV in conven-
ing synods at the Lateran.[45] That may be so, but it must be recalled that
Hadrian reigned until 1159, four years after Arnold's execution. The question of the frequency of papal councils requires further examination, moving
beyond specific political issues to the institutional development of the
Roman see.

The link between the Innocentian party in the 1130 schism and the work
of Gratian has been examined recently.[46] Whether or not this side of the
dispute is reflected in the *Concordia discordantium canonum,* that compilation probably achieved final form near the end of Innocent's pontificate. The second quarter of the twelfth century was the transitional period
in Church law between the *ius antiquum* and the *ius novum,* an evolution

symbolized and indeed defined by the emergence of Gratian's *Concordia* (or *Decretum*).

Conceived as a universal treatise on the institutions and problems of canon law, the book used the whole of the traditional *auctoritates* handed down in the earlier collections [i.e., the *ius antiquum*] as material from which to draw, point for point, the textual arguments for the canonical doctrines Gratian proposed. . . . The definitive *dossier* of canonical authorities of the past had become established in this book. . . . The checkered variety of law-producing agencies that had vexed earlier generations faded away, since from the struggles of the Gregorian era and the ensuing clarification of thought, the papacy had emerged as the undisputed guardian and master of the law, the sole agency which henceforth in its supreme magisterial, judicial, and legislative pronouncements would make truly "common," general law. This new papal law [i.e., the *ius novum*] appeared in the thousands of rulings that flowed from the papal Chancery since the mid-twelfth century, settling thousands of new problems and cases.[47]

The Roman pontiff was becoming in fact as well as in theory the prime legal arbiter of Latin Christendom, and the dispatch of papal decretal letters—the instruments of centralized administration and justice—increased throughout the twelfth century under Eugene III, Hadrian IV, and especially Alexander III.[48]

Not everyone applauded this. Writing in the *De consideratione* (ca. 1150), to his Cistercian disciple Pope Eugene III, St. Bernard of Clairvaux questioned the pontiff's deep involvement in hearing and deciding litigation.

I ask you, what about this: from morning to evening personally involved with cases, or hearing the cases of others? . . . The nights are not free. You hardly have time to sleep enough . . . before it is necessary to rise for contentions. . . . I am certain that you deplore this state of affairs also, but that is in vain if you do not strive to alter it. . . . What can be more degrading and unworthy, especially for the Roman pontiff, than to labor, I do not say every day but nearly every hour, with such matters? When do you pray? When do you teach people? When do you build up the Church? When do you meditate on the Law? Indeed, laws make a great din in the palace daily, but it is the law of Justinian, not of the Lord. Is that just? You might say, "Truly, 'the law of the Lord is pure, converting the soul'," but these are not so much laws as wranglings and sophistry, subverting the power of judgment.[49]

St. Bernard notwithstanding, such centralization helps to account for the decline in papal conciliar activity which occurred by the middle of the twelfth century. Affairs which earlier might have been brought before councils now were settled by curial decision. Synodal conclaves were less essential. The decretal letter was supplanting the grand meetings of pope, bishops, and abbots.[50]

But crises still demanded the public forum and solicitude available in councils, as the turmoil of the 1130s and the early 1160s proved. Following the Victorine synod of September 1162, it was not at all surprising to find Alexander planning to counter with an impressive gathering.[51] Disturbing pronouncements about such assemblies from the imperial camp might have intensified that desire. Frederick was employing the term "general council," and similar expressions, for synods which originated with him.[52] This contradicted canonical tradition. The *Summa Parisiensis,* dating from just about the middle of the twelfth century, put it this way: "It should be recognized . . . that a general council is one constituted either in the presence of the pope or his legate or in some other way by papal authority, for example through letters, and only this (type of council) can make canons or depose bishops."[53] Similar assessments are to be found elsewhere.[54] But the emperor reportedly opened the council in 1160 at Pavia with the following remarks:

Although I know that through the office and dignity of the empire the power to convoke councils is mine, especially in (time of) such great dangers to the Church—for this is known to have been done by the emperors Constantine, Theodosius, Justinian, and more recently Charlemagne and Otto—nevertheless, I commit to you and to your power the authority to define this supremely important business. . . .[55]

Alexander already had presided at one synod. Several weeks after he landed in France a group of clerics met with him in a council at Montpellier.[56] This assembly was in session on May 17, and writing on that day to the bishop of Verona, Alexander mentioned the presence of the archbishops of Sens, Tours, Aix, and Narbonne, and the bishops of Auxerre, St.-Malo, Nevers, Thérouanne, Montpellier, and Toulon. He was expecting the archbishops of Bourges and Reims, as well as Cardinals Henry and William with the bishops of Évreux and Bayeux, who were envoys of King Henry II.[57] Three weeks later, in a letter to the archbishop of Genoa, Alexander again listed clerics received at Montpellier.[58] Those bishops already designated were repeated, with the addition of the bishop of Autun; also added, and specified as appearing after May 17, were the archbishop of Bourges and the bishops of Clermont, Périgueux, Cahors, Chartres, Nîmes, and Évreux, plus the bishop of Oviedo, whom the pope himself consecrated on May 20. Alexander also mentioned unnamed messengers of Henry II, and Peter, King Louis VII's brother, who is indicated as being present on the 17th. Others included only in this second letter also must have participated in the council, assuming that it lasted more than a day.

These details in letters to Italy reveal the pontiff's sensitivity about his reception in France, and a desire to publicize his acceptance. But the council in Montpellier was not large. Despite promulgating decrees, it apparently made no legislative impact.[59] Alexander needed to do more, and after his meetings with Kings Henry and Louis in the Loire Valley additional things would have been possible. It has even been speculated that the participants in that obscure colloquy "planned a council, which met at Tours in May 1163 and turned into an impressive demonstration in favour of Alexander."[60]

## CONCILIAR PREPARATIONS

An elaborate council was pondered by Alexander and his royal adherents, either in person or through intermediaries,[61] for a papal letter to King Alphonso II of Aragon indicates such deliberations with Henry and Louis.[62] Writing to the Spanish ruler on 7 December 1162, Alexander announced his safe residence at Tours. With the concurrence of the kings of England and France and "the entire French Church," he has decided to convoke a great synod in that city. Alphonso is urged to cooperate. Let him receive kindly the papal subdeacon P., who is journeying to Aragon to summon the clergy, and let him not jeopardize their attendance but rather advocate it. No doubt it was about the same time that Alexander sent a subdeacon named Octavian to Ireland with a similar invitation.[63]

Even in the unlikely event that the pope did not discuss his plans with Henry II face to face, this ruler's support was crucial. Tours was situated in Henry's domain, although in territory which theoretically he held from the French king.[64] There was scant hope that English churchmen could attend without royal approval, despite what had happened in 1148 when Archbishop Theobald of Canterbury went to the Council of Reims against the wishes of King Stephen.[65] Probably simultaneously with the legations to Aragon and Ireland, Alexander dispatched another subdeacon, this time a man named Theodin, to England.[66] Ralph of Diceto reported that, with the king's permission, Theodin summoned the archbishops, bishops, abbots, and priors of the land to Tours.[67]

Charles Duggan has written, "The twelfth century was not an age of unconditional surrender: victory of Church or monarchy on one point did not necessarily entail the same result on others."[68] Alexander gained Henry's consent for a council at Tours, but it was not simply to be assumed that the English clergy would come. From the beginning of his reign, Henry II was intent on controlling the Church at least to the extent of safeguarding what he deemed to be royal interests.[69] On 18 March 1163, Alexander wrote to him in response to a letter received.[70] The king had not taken lightly the matter of releasing English prelates for Tours. According to the pope, Henry's letter related that such permission had been granted only after an assembly of archbishops, bishops, earls (*comites*), and barons.[71] To eliminate the possibility of action prejudicial to the crown at the upcoming synod, Alexander now promised that no *new customs* would thence be introduced into the kingdom (*nova consuetudo in regnum tuum*), nor would its *dignity* (*ipsius regni dignitas*) be diminished in any way.[72]

This concession is reminiscent of the Constitutions of Clarendon (January 1164), with their repeated emphasis on *customs* and *dignities,* and the entire episode also recalls Ordericus Vitalis's rendition of the instructions given by Henry I to the English clerics embarking for Calixtus II's Council of Reims in 1119:

[He] permitted the prelates . . . to attend . . . but absolutely forbade that they should raise any complaints against one another. For he said, "I will render full justice to all who seek it in my realm. I pay the yearly revenue to the Roman Church arranged by my predecessors, and likewise I hold the privileges conceded to me from earlier times. Go, greet the pope for me, and humbly hear the apostolic decrees. But do not introduce superfluous innovations into my kingdom."[73]

It is unlikely that Alexander spontaneously would have proffered such regard for English royal tradition. It must have been elicited by Henry, with an eye toward his grandfather's days, as the condition for releasing his clergy. Once at Tours, these churchmen took their monarch's attitude seriously, as is evident in an episode described from an earlier source by Matthew Paris:[74] the abbot of St. Albans quarreled at the synod with his counterpart from Bury St. Edmunds about seating; yet no formal accusations were made, "since King Henry II of England had forbidden all the prelates of his realm to bring any dispute on any matter before the Curia."

There seems to be no basis for assuming that Thomas Becket was instrumental in persuading Henry to tolerate his clerics' acceptance of the conciliar invitation.[75] Such reluctance need not be postulated, provided that certain assurances were forthcoming.[76] Henry would have realized that his position was a commanding one. The pope was anxious to make the council as impressive as possible, and a sizable English contingent would help. The king, perhaps recalling Beauvais in 1160,[77] knew that the pontiff was a man who would bargain. If politics is the art of the possible, both principals in this drama were politicians. As has been said so well about Alexander, the pope was a "theorist of expediency."[78]

Alphonso of Aragon had been informed that the kings of both England and France backed the synodal project. Henry's approval was crucial if Tours were to be more than a repetition of the gathering at Montpellier. But the constant support of Louis VII must not be underestimated, even if the evolution of the preparations is obscure. Early in November 1162, Alexander dispatched to Louis his closest adviser, Cardinal-bishop Bernard of Porto.[79] His mission is unclear, and the papal letter of introduction is veiled.[80] Alexander wrote at the same time to Louis's brother, Archbishop Henry of Reims, soliciting his aid in Bernard's unspecified project.[81] Henry was asked to employ his influence in promoting "whatever is expedient for the Church of God at this time, especially in this kingdom. . . . You should go to the king and readily endeavor to accomplish what our bishop proposes. . . ." This could have included matters related to the council.[82]

By December 8, Alexander was willing to write openly to the French king about the synod.[83] He informed him that royal messengers had been received kindly, and were being sent back with a considered response to the topics raised. The pope did not delineate the issues nor his reply, noting that elaboration was unnecessary since the envoys could relate his stance.[84] Alexander expressed the belief that Bishop Maurice of Paris had informed Louis both about the council (*de celebratione concilii*) and about the proposed papal trip to the Île-de-France (which occurred in the spring of 1163, before the synod).[85] But in case these things had not been ventilated fully in Maurice's report, they were included in the account which the messenger would deliver.

Such vagueness bears little analysis. Alexander hardly would write to Aragon on December 7 that he had the support of the English and French crowns if Louis's first knowledge of the conciliar enterprise were Maurice's report, which the pontiff was not sure had been received in full by December 8. Louis must have known about the project from the earliest stages, surely before the letter to Alphonso. That the first discussion occurred in the conference at Chouzy/Chouzé is uncertain, but plausible.

One episode reveals Louis involved in the preparations. At an undetermined date prior to the synod, he addressed a letter both to Girard, treasurer of St.-Martin's in Tours, and to the burghers of the town. The issue was prices being charged for lodgings.[86] The king had learned that with the council in view, accommodations were being overpriced (*de conducendis hospitiis pro concilio non servatur mensura*). Louis's reprimand to the treasurer at St.-Martin's implicates that section of town known as Châteauneuf—the mercantile settlement that had grown around the great church. The treasurer was its temporal administrator, but the monarch, in his honorific capacity as abbot of St.-Martin's, was the seigneur. The residents of this district, who had banded into a commune in the mid-twelfth century, must have hoped for a quick profit from the impending council. Perhaps the chapter at St.-Martin's cooperated with them, for it was unlikely that a similar opportunity would arise again soon. Louis set the price for "more expensive lodgings" (*carius hospitium*) at six pounds. This was a maximum, according to which other facilities were to be priced, based on their quality. How widespread was the problem, and were such controls effective? It is impossible to answer either question. The letter illustrates only a part of one instance of what must have been a recurring situation—the economic stresses and opportunities offered by large councils[87]—and the survival of other, similar documents would illuminate a hazy yet persistent aspect of conciliar history.

The assembly which Alexander III was preparing for Tours would not be this town's first papal council. Nearly seven decades earlier, in 1096, Pope Urban II convened a synod in St.-Martin's, perhaps because the cathedral of St.-Maurice was decrepit.[88] By the middle of the twelfth century it had been rebuilt,[89] and in that church, on 19 May 1163, Alexander opened his carefully planned gathering, probably with great expectations.[90]

# 2

---

# Conciliar Organization, I

## THE SERMONS

The procedures used in medieval councils, especially those prior to the thirteenth century, are difficult to retrieve. Although some study of conciliar organization has been done for eleventh- and twelfth-century papal and English provincial gatherings, much remains to be discovered.[1] Foreville has employed an *Ordo Romanus qualiter concilium agatur,* from the twelfth-century Roman Pontifical, as a likely guide to the events at the 1179 Lateran Council.[2] Synods began with liturgical solemnities. This *Ordo* calls for opening prayers, a Gospel reading, and singing of the *Veni creator spiritus.* The presiding bishop might then deliver a sermon, either on the Biblical lesson or on something else deemed appropriate "to moral instruction and discipline." With his permission, other clerics also could preach.

Similar events occurred at Innocent III's Lateran Council in 1215.[3] On the first day at dawn, the pope celebrated mass in the presence of the cardinals, archbishops, and bishops. These prelates plus the abbots then were seated, the latter unmitred and apparently brought into the basilica only after the eucharistic liturgy. A throng of lower clergy and laymen then were admitted. The pope, situated with the cardinals and his other officials (*ministri*) on a dais of unspecified location, intoned the *Veni creator,* which was taken up by the assembly. After the collect, Innocent began his opening address, but it was difficult to hear because of the noisy crowd.[4] This sermon was followed by another from the Patriarch of Jerusalem: one of the main accomplishments of the synod would be the proclamation of a new crusade.

Although liturgical details are lacking, analogous ceremonies must have taken place at Tours. What survive are glimpses of the sermonizing. Inaugural speeches were an important conciliar tradition, for they could establish a general tone and even summarize the proposed legislation.[5] But aside from a copy of one such address, transmitted independently, the

12

homiletical information relevant to Tours is complicated by the nature of its source—a lengthy poem entitled the *Draco Normannicus*. The historical worth of this verse history of the house of Anjou is problematic.[6] Completed in 1169 by a monk at Bec known as Stephen of Rouen, it has been characterized in the following way by one of its editors:

We see that the poem furnishes facts hitherto unknown; that it gives an independent view of the great controversies of the day; that it lends support to statements hitherto without confirmation; and, finally, that it gives us an indirect assurance that no events of primary importance for the history of the years from 1153 to 1169 are absolutely lost.[7]

On the other hand:

No more choice contribution to English history could perhaps have been made than an account of these years, had the poet been less diffuse, and less intent on turning tricky verses. Fortunately it is impossible for the vainest and most shallow of mankind to write about the days in which he lived, without unintentionally telling much that is exceedingly valuable to after ages. This is the case with the anonymous [*sic*] author of the *Draco Normannicus*. Three-fourths of that which he wishes most to impress upon his readers is valueless; but the remainder, and the whole of his chance utterances, are deeply interesting.[8]

The difficulties begin early in the presentation, when Stephen seems unsure whether the council might not have convened at Reims![9] Since the poem appears to have survived in a single fifteenth-century manuscript, this mistake may not be the author's and should not be belabored.[10] Stephen was "implacably hostile" to Thomas Becket,[11] and offered an unflattering description of him at the synod, to be considered in due course.[12] He cared little for papal aggrandizement, and generally portrayed Alexander III "as arrogant and greedy."[13] But he may have attended the council, and certainly would have talked to people who did; hence what is related about the assembly and its participants merits consideration. It is the *Draco,* for example, which records that a secondary reason for the gathering—the primary one being the schism—was Alexander's penury.[14] "The papal court delights in the resplendence of metallic luster":[15] this line both recalls a common object of medieval satire—curial venality—and betrays Stephen's bias. But when the pope is termed a "poor exile,"[16] and when special attention is devoted to the abundant funds which the English clergy brought to Tours,[17] the author is reflecting the reduced circumstances of Alexander's sojourn in France. Stephen divulged that the kings of England and France sent to the council special gifts for the pope. One contributed a thousand gold coins and the other a jeweled cloak (who gave what is unclear).[18]

The *Draco's* report of the sermons is tantalizing.[19] Seven addresses are indicated, but only one is elaborated—a speech by Alexander delivered at the final session, which culminated in an excommunication of Victor IV. Stephen even recounts what he thought the pontiff had or should have said in this instance.[20] The notices of the remaining six discourses, including another by the pope, stand at the beginning of the account. Alexander spoke first, "polished in the Roman manner."[21] He was followed by the Cardinal-priests William of S. Pietro in Vincoli, "gleaming with words," and Henry of SS. Nereo e Achilleo, "brilliant with flowery rhetoric," then Archbishops Hugh of Rouen and Roger of York, and finally Bishop Arnulf of Lisieux, on whom more shortly. Between Roger and Arnulf, Stephen inserted a curious remark about Thomas Becket, explaining that he remained silent because he was not well-versed in speaking Latin. Thomas's oral facility in this language in 1163 cannot be ascertained.[22] But even if Stephen was correct, the archbishop would not be the last English prelate of his time whose Latinity proved embarrassing before the pope and cardinals.[23]

Three of the designated speakers, the two cardinals and Archbishop Hugh, had been important figures in the negotiations for recognition of Alexander in England and France.[24] Cardinal William, who probably was the shrewdest politician at Alexander's disposal, Cardinal Henry, and Cardinal-deacon Otto of S. Nicolao in Carcere Tulliano were the Alexandrian spokesmen at Beauvais.[25] Hugh of Rouen, in all likelihood, also was there;[26] but even if not, he performed the crucial marriage of the English prince and the French princess after the cardinals had arranged the dispensation.[27] Those affairs could have influenced the roles of these men at Tours, where their activity might have been intended to demonstrate publicly that rancor about the marital episode was past. Furthermore, Hugh may have been the oldest bishop in terms of episcopal service at the council, having gained his see at Rouen in 1130.[28] Such venerability could have recommended him as a speaker.

According to Stephen of Rouen, Alexander "permitted" (*cessit*) Arnulf of Lisieux to preach to the assembly.[29] Did the pope recognize him in an offhand manner during the initial session, or, as is more likely, had he been designated previously to deliver one of the keynote addresses? As Arnulf recounted it, there is no room for doubt. The pontiff had enjoined him to speak, and would that the honor had befallen a more worthy, more knowledgeable, and more eloquent man.[30] His sermon from that great occasion— or at least a sermon which he was able to circulate under that rubric— survives. As preserved in one tradition, it is divided into two parts.[31] These sections mention explicitly that they were not for the same day. Stephen related that Arnulf rambled on and on—"a roaring river flowing from the depths of its source"—and was barely able to be stopped by cries and by hand signals.[32] Conceivably, his torrent of verbiage necessitated his continuing at another session, a fact that he may have incorporated into the published text by dividing it, as will be discussed.

Discounting the final discourse by the pope, perhaps Stephen has compressed into one list the inaugural preachers at successive plenary sittings of the council. By doubling Arnulf's contribution, the number of addresses thus proposed as sessional is seven. Although information lacks about its closing date, if we follow this construct, and assume one general convocation a day, the synod sat for at least a week.[33] But apart from the pope and the two cardinals, in whose orations Stephen took particular delight, he mentioned only speeches by Anglo-Norman prelates—the archbishops of York and Rouen, and the bishop of Lisieux. Is it likely that no French delegates other than Normans spoke?[34] Perhaps Stephen recorded only those non-Roman preachers whom he knew or who were from Normandy or England, or maybe he simply was constructing a very pointed snub for Thomas Becket. York, Rouen, and even Lisieux could have their bishops harangue the assembly, but venerable Canterbury could not, for its incumbent "was not well instructed in speaking Latin."[35]

The survival of Arnulf's sermon is a minor but comforting point for Stephen of Rouen's accuracy (notwithstanding his possible mistake about the council's site). Bishop Arnulf has been characterized variously by modern writers. Knowles saw him, in view of his actions in the Becket dispute, as a man "of doubtful reputation," and concluded that "it is difficult to acquit him of double-dealing."[36] Frank Barlow, who edited and wrote a long introduction to his correspondence, observed that for Arnulf "the full man enjoyed the spoils of both worlds, and such ambition was to be expected in a man whose relatives had been both bishops and royal officials. . . . He was to live through difficult times when compromise was necessary for existence."[37] Very recently, Beryl Smalley described him as "a gifted rhetor and publicist."[38] Arnulf had been well educated, including a period in Italy studying law.[39] After 1159 and the dual papal election, he was an enthusiastic advocate of Alexander,[40] loyalty perhaps rewarded by the chance to speak at Tours. Barlow has discerned "a strain of arrogance" and "a note of pomposity" in the bishop's character,[41] which might help to explain the verbal gusher unleashed for that occasion.

Sometime after the council, Arnulf wrote to Giles of La Perche, archdeacon at Rouen, regarding the circulation of a written version of his speech.[42] Since Giles became bishop at Évreux in 1170,[43] the letter dates within seven years of the synod. Arnulf related that he had been urged to publish the address by several people seated near him during its delivery, but who had not heard clearly due to the noisy crowd. He hesitated to comply because of the difference between an oration and its transcription, and begged Giles's charitable indulgence when reading the imperfect work before him.

Two printed versions of the text exist. One presents it in two parts, the other in one. Reuter argued that it was a single presentation, and that the divided form might offer sketches for the sermon actually delivered.[44] The matter requires a study of the many manuscripts catalogued in Barlow's edition of the letters, but the following observations can be made. The address seemingly was printed first, in 1585, by C. Mignault, as part of an edition of Arnulf's letters based on Paris, Bibliothèque nationale MS lat. 14763.[45] This rendition, which was continuous and undivided, was reproduced in the following century in the different editions of M. de La Bigne's *Bibliotheca veterum patrum,* and also came to Baronius.[46] From the *Annales* it passed into the conciliar collections, from Binius through the other seventeenth- and eighteenth-century compilations to Mansi.[47] The second printed edition was made in the last century by J. A. Giles.[48] Using Oxford, St. John's College MS 126, Giles offered a text which is split into two parts.[49] The first designates itself *Hodiernus sermo*; the second opens by recalling what was said *Hesterno sermone.* Since Arnulf spoke only of a *sermo* in his letter to Giles of La Perche, this division could be an alteration rendered after the text left the author's hands. But another possibility, already noted, would be to postulate an originally undivided address, which the verbose bishop was forced to extend over two sessions. Such a termination and new beginning may have been incorporated by Arnulf into the published discourse, even while he continued to conceive of it integrally. Later, the separation could have been obliterated in certain manuscripts.

The work is decidedly an exercise in rhetoric, devoted more to homiletical technique than to informative or profound analyses. How closely what was published resembles what was said cannot be determined. It apparently was similar enough for Arnulf to think that it would be accepted by those who heard the oral version; but recalling the din accompanying the sermon's delivery, perhaps such consistency was less important than might be imagined. Barlow has observed that "Arnulf considered that the chief merit of his productions lay in their style."[50] Whatever changes were made probably had stylistic considerations in view, a possibility which is hardly comforting to anyone considering the address as a historical witness for the synod.

Toward the end of the letter to Giles, Arnulf related that because of the onslaught at that time against the liberty of the Church of God, his sermon conscientiously (*diligentius*) treated questions of unity and liberty.[51] Following a tedious introduction about the qualifications of a good preacher, these themes are introduced.

Without these two the Church cannot be safe nor indeed exist, because unless the Church has unity, it will not be one. If it is not one, it will not be. Everything that is exists because it is unitary. What is not integral loses substance as well as unity. Likewise, unless it (the Church) has liberty, it will be wretched. But wretchedness for it is equivalent to non-existence. Indeed, it is worse for it to be miserable than not to be. . . . Therefore, my dearest lords and brothers, so that the state of the Church can be preserved unharmed, it is necessary solicitously to provide for its unity and liberty. For in these days, during this storm, we have seen with sorrow that both of these are pursued by many misfortunes and attacked by manifold injuries. The ambition of the schismatics endeavors to tear the former; the violence of tyrants seeks to destroy the latter.[52]

Notwithstanding the tautologies, Arnulf is expressing what was important to the Alexandrians—the tragedy of schism, yet the necessity for ecclesiastical self-determination. It is one formulation of the paradox about societal order which had vexed Latin Christendom since the eleventh century. But if unity and liberty are integral to the Church's existence, it is, according to Arnulf, because of divine institution. A Church structured thus is inviolable, and that transcendent constitution will assure an ultimate triumph for those gathered at Tours.[53] The bishop from Lisieux reminded the council fathers that

it is impossible to rip the spiritual sacrament (*spirituale sacramentum*) of ecclesiastical unity,[54] which was established and confirmed by the Father in an unbreachable covenant between Christ and the Church. It is impossible to withdraw from the Church of God its liberty, consecrated by the effusion of the Lord's blood. Although the chaff from the Lord's threshing floor is beaten away by the winnowing fan of inconsistency and vanity, because of its absence the produce (*fructus*) of the floor is not lessened but purged. Likewise, although the princes of darkness vehemently rise up against the Church of God, the gates of hell cannot prevail against it.[55]

The Alexandrians "ought to labor with utmost charity for the return of those who are outside,"[56] but this reconciliation must be a penitent reintegration into "our unity," not a compromise.[57] In one of the most interesting passages in the speech, Arnulf emphasized the duty to work for an end to the schism, and offered at the same time some thoughts about the rewards and obligations of the pastoral office.

We are bishops, thus we wish to be sanctified by ecclesiastical sacraments, to be endowed with benefices, and to be distinguished by honors. For this reason, we obtain here the first seats in the council,[58] the prime places at banquets, and acclamations in public. For the same reason, multitudes turn toward us so that from our hand they might receive a part of the blessing committed to us. They seek to receive from our plenitude what we have received from the fullness of Christ.[59]

This pattern for the descent of blessing, from heaven to earth through the Church, is reiterated by a curious exegesis of the head-beard-garment imagery of Psalm 132:2, which Arnulf refers to Christ, the clergy, and the populace respectively.[60]

If what was published reflects what was said, this exaltation of episcopal collegiality undoubtedly flattered many of the bishops who heard it, although the concomitant sentiments of the council's more than four hundred abbots would be interesting.[61] Throughout the sermon, however, neither the papal office nor the circumstances of Alexander's election are mentioned. Arnulf was, of course, only one of several speakers, including the pope, and not the best received according to the *Draco*. But there is no reason to interpret his discourse as even a veiled challenge to the pontiff. Just the opposite explanation is preferable.

Despite the rhetoric about unity and liberty, everyone in the synod knew that the present conflict reduced to the matter of Alexander's papal claims. These, of course, were not openly in question at Tours,[62] although Stephen of Rouen mentioned that Alexander did recount the issues at the end of the council, prefatory to anathematizing the Victorines, excluding Frederick.[63] The *Draco*'s version of that address cannot be trusted, but its delivery is probable,[64] and other sources corroborate Frederick's omission from the condemnations.[65] Since no hint of the content of the other orations is available, it is impossible to fit Arnulf's into a program. But could not the intention of the bishop from Lisieux have been to solidify clerical and especially episcopal backing for Alexander, through a blend of flattery and traditional ecclesiology? This course might have seemed wiser than reciting the pope's claims and problems, which everyone knew, and which Alexander himself intended to analyze.

Writing to King Alphonso of Aragon, Alexander had stated that at Tours he planned to establish "what we have recognized, the Lord revealing, as pertinent to the honor of God, the exaltation of the Church, and the salvation and peace of all."[66] The Church's exaltation and universal spiritual prosperity might be considered synonymous with ecclesiastical liberty and unity. But for those gathered at Tours, the strength and even the meaning of these concepts depended on their pope's survival. The chief reason for the council was to offer an impressive display of support for Alexander, and to emphasize that the Church was operating under his guidance. As Reuter observed, the gathering was "a lever in his hand, to enhance his sphere of power (*Machtstellung*)."[67] Arnulf's sermon, with its confident appeal to a sympathetic audience, represents one facet of the conciliar program. Others, of a less propagandist sort, will emerge in the following chapters.

*While the present volume was in press the author became aware of the text of another sermon which may have originated in the Council of Tours. The authorship and origin of that homily remain to be determined, and must be reserved for a special study.*

# 3

## Conciliar Organization, II

### THE PARTICIPANTS

Both previous chapters emphasized Pope Alexander's desire for a great council as a display of strength, and Chapter 2 noted Arnulf of Lisieux's appeal to the bishops thus convened at Tours. Who was in that group? This question assumes more than routine importance, considering the tensions which had engulfed Europe by 1163, and happily it can be answered in detail. Specific evidence about the political mood of the assembled council fathers is lacking, but some conjectures can be made. The majority should be regarded as sympathetic to the Alexandrian cause, and openly hostile clerics probably either did not come or were refused admission. Yet there is no reason to exclude the possibility that some skeptics could be found in attendance, particularly from regions outside the influence of Kings Henry and Louis. It seems unlikely, however, that such doubters as there were would remain at Tours and not capitulate. The pressure to conform must have been overwhelming, especially in view of the condemnation of Victor and his supporters.

Membership in such gatherings appears to have had a canonical as well as a political dimension, and those who attended must have been obligated to abide by the legislation enacted. The wariness of English monarchs toward their clergy's participation in foreign synods, whence they might feel compelled to introduce troublesome novelties into the realm, has been mentioned.[1] Early in the twelfth century, St. Anselm more than once wrote that he could not shrink from attacking lay investiture, after having heard the pope condemn it in a council.[2] The archbishop is recalling Urban II's assembly at St. Peter's in 1099, where he was a celebrity.[3] Furthermore, churchmen who witnessed the drafting and promulgating of conciliar statutes could feel specially informed about their meaning. Consider a letter written to Bishop Ulger of Angers between 1125 and 1132 by Abbot Geoffrey

19

of Vendôme.[4] Its subject was a ruling from the Council of Clermont in 1095, defining certain financial arrangements between bishops and monasteries.[5] Geoffrey insisted on his particular reading of this controversial decree,[6] and chided Ulger that "you did not participate in that council and I did."[7] The abbot wanted to convey the impression that his knowledge of the canon, because he had been at Clermont, was better than that of someone who had not been there: Ulger had to rely on accounts of the legislation, but Geoffrey had witnessed its promulgation.[8] Although "facts about methods of drafting and authorizing canons are unfortunately scarce," and in this regard "the historian is bound to raise more questions than he can answer,"[9] the consequences of attendance at a synod merit close examination.

It is difficult, however, to trace the actual participants at medieval councils, especially those held prior to 1179. What lists have survived for assemblies before the Lateran Council of that year appear, for the most part, to be unofficial, and certainly are incomplete.[10] Three papal councils—Clermont, 1095; Lateran, 1112; and Pisa, 1135—can be used to illustrate the fragmentary inventories that are extant for this period.

A group of names survives from Clermont, including 18 bishops, appended to a rendition of a conciliar judgment for the house of Marmoutier.[11] This is a private document, undoubtedly intended for the monastery's archives, and offers an incomplete record of the council fathers. Perhaps it is even a partial enumeration of the witnesses at the session, for the compiler may have named only those whom he recognized or later could remember. The *Gesta* from 1112 derive from Pope Paschal II's register, and can therefore claim some sort of authority.[12] They describe events on the fourth, fifth, and sixth days of the council. On the sixth and final day, the pope and the assembled prelates condemned "that privilege (*privilegium*) which is not a privilege, but truly ought to be called a depravity (*pravilegium*)"[13]—the right of investiture extorted from Paschal in 1111 by the emperor Henry V.[14] After this denunciation was read by Bishop Gerald of Angoulême, it was acclaimed by the gathering. The *Gesta* terminate with a list of witnesses, adding others not present for that session but who were concurrently in Rome and later consented. Approximately 50 people are designated, although the total number of bishops at the synod was nearly 130.[15] The record for Pisa offers more information than either of the others. It survives in the introduction to an abbreviated version of the conciliar proceedings, and is the most extensive known attendance catalogue for a papal synod before 1179. Although edited since the last century, the account recently has been studied thoroughly and reedited by Dieter Girgensohn. It is only a private document,[16] but nonetheless it records 122 bishops.

In his *Vita* of Alexander III, Cardinal Boso tabulated the participants at Tours. Together with the pope, the assembly included 17 cardinals, 124 abbots, and a throng of others, both clerics and laymen.[17] These figures should be taken seriously. Although no longer chamberlain under Alexander, Boso, as an important member of the papal entourage and a likely conciliar eyewitness, would have had access to reliable information.[18] His rendition of the canons probably was copied from official documents, and his attendance figures may derive from the same source.[19]

Some other comments on the participants at Tours can be summarized. An anonymous chronicler from Laon erroneously placed both the English and French monarchs there, and mentioned the presence of bishops from all of France.[20] John of Cornwall, opening a discussion of the assembly's heated Christological debates, spoke in general terms of the clergy from England and France.[21] Ralph of Diceto is more informative, at least about the English, writing that three bishops—Winchester, Lincoln, and Bath— were excused because of illness.[22] Romuald of Salerno recorded archbishops, bishops, and abbots from England, Scotland, Ireland, Spain, and France;[23] and a chronicler from St.-Aubin in Angers listed France, Burgundy, Spain, Aquitaine, England, Normandy, and Brittany.[24]

Hugh of Poitiers, in the *Liber de libertate monasterii Vizeliacensis,* offered quantitative detail.[25] All of the bishops, 105 of them, from the provinces of Lyons, Narbonne, Vienne, Bourges, Sens, Reims, Rouen, Tours, Bordeaux, Auch, and the Pennine and Maritime Alps came to Tours. He added Canterbury, York, Scotland, and Ireland, but did not enumerate the bishops. Following a remark about non-episcopal clerics,[26] Hugh related that many Germans wrote secretly to Alexander professing their obedience, and that a not inconsiderable number of Italians were present, some through written communications, others in person.

In a letter written just after the event, to the bishops in the province of Salzburg, the pope spoke in non-specific but lavish terms:[27] "We celebrated a magnificent and solemn council. Elderly men, who customarily have attended councils in the north, confirm that none of our predecessors for forty years is known to have celebrated a greater or more solemn synod."[28] This is tantalizing, but not as lucid as it could be. Does Alexander mean that venerable men who had attended councils in the north, *and also in Italy,* have attested that no such assembly, *in either region,* in the past forty years was more spectacular than Tours? Or is he claiming that no synod *in the north* in the last four decades was greater? The chronological span might suggest the former, since forty years before 1163 was 1123, the date of Calixtus II's great Lateran Council. But could Tours have outranked in Alexander's mind Innocent II's synod at Pisa in 1135, or especially the same pope's assembly at the Lateran in 1139?[29] If Alexander had in view only meetings north of the Alps, the "forty years" might refer back to 1119, and Calixtus's synods at Reims and Toulouse. Those could have been the earliest papal

councils held outside of Italy which anyone in 1163 would remember from
personal experience, although it is possible that people still were alive who
had attended Paschal II's Council of Troyes in 1107. But whether or not
Alexander was recalling a specific event, his intention is clear. He was anxious to enhance the importance of the synod at Tours, and to impress his
readers with the widespread support which he had mustered there. As
already noted, no official figures exist for the papal assemblies between 1123
and 1163 to facilitate comparisons.[30] But Alexander's boasting aside, Tours
was a substantial gathering, and the event must have rankled Frederick
Barbarossa and Victor IV.


BISHOPS

It now is possible to ascertain which bishops were there, for a detailed list
of the episcopal participants has survived. It is a curious document, bearing
no heading, written on the verso of the final page (fol. 16) of the *Annales
Cicestrenses,* which are apparently preserved uniquely in British Library MS
Cotton Vitellius A XVII.[31] Apart from four thirteenth-century supplements,
the *Annales* date from the middle of the twelfth century. The final entries,
up to the year 1164, where the twelfth-century hand ends, are therefore
contemporary with the events recorded. Among the last of those remarks,
the item for 1162 notes Thomas Becket's promotion to Canterbury, and the
council at Tours. The sole observation for 1163 reports that "King Henry
is angry with Archbishop Thomas of Canterbury and all the English clergy
. . ."; the rest of the line has been erased. Mention of Victor IV's death
follows for 1164, together with "Archbishop Thomas is exiled." The *Annales*
then end, on fol. 16r, except for the thirteenth-century additions.

On 16v, in a twelfth-century hand, is a list of bishops. They are not designated by proper names, but by sees—*Cenomannensis,* etc.—and are arranged generally according to ecclesiastical provinces, although a few head-
ings such as *De Hispania* occur. Portions of the text are badly faded, but
all the names can be deciphered. It is unquestionably an attendance list:
*De provincia Turonensi, ipse archiepiscopus, et cum eo. . . .* Walther Holtzmann had noticed the page while he was preparing the *Papsturkunden in
England.* He commented on the absence of German names, and conjectured
that the report pertained to the Council of Tours.[32] This identification is certain beyond all doubt.

Aside from the lack of German entries, and the fact that the province
of Tours begins the list,[33] the chronological terminus of the *Annales* fits
Holtzmann's conjecture. More significantly, however, Ralph of Diceto's
information about the English contingent at Tours accords with the new

catalogue: Winchester, Lincoln, and Bath are missing (as are Hereford and Carlisle, both of which were vacant in 1163).[34] With the exception of Ireland and the province of Vienne, both to be considered below, the geographical range of the manuscript's list is consistent with the comments about participation already noted from writers such as Hugh of Poitiers. Ralph of Diceto also related that York's only suffragan at the assembly was Durham.[35] Under the heading *De provincia Eboracensi,* the new text confirms that.[36]

Consider further those sees designated as occupied by an *electus*—Worcester, Dol, and Santiago de Compostela. (1) Roger of Gloucester was chosen bishop of Worcester in March 1163—the council met in May—but remained unconsecrated until August 1164.[37] (2) John IV of Dol possessed his see in 1163, but as late as 1170 still was *electus,*[38] by reason of the protracted struggle between Tours and Dol for metropolitan jurisdiction over Brittany. Judgments in the quarrel repeatedly were given for Tours; in 1161, for example, Pope Alexander prescribed that the bishop-elect of Dol had to be consecrated by and promise obedience to Tours.[39] An uncooperative candidate obviously would remain *electus.* (3) The case of Compostela is more obscure.[40] A schism arose there in 1160 between Archbishop Martin, the ruler of the church since 1156 but then expelled, and successive royal replacements styled *electi.*[41] The *electus Compostellanus* in 1163 was named Peter. Although already both bishop of Monoñedo and royal *maiordomus* to King Fernando II of León, this man would have led the Compostellan delegation to Tours.

One hundred and eighteen names are recorded in the new account, including two sees represented by legates—Béziers and Nîmes—and excluding three cardinal-bishops placed at the end *De curia*—Ostia, Porto, and Albano. Boso counted 124 bishops at Tours, apparently exclusive of cardinals, whom he mentioned separately.[42] The enumeration in the manuscript differs, therefore, only by six (or eight, depending on how Boso handled Béziers and Nîmes) from what can be taken as an official count.

Hugh of Poitiers's total of 105 bishops in the council, from twelve provinces including the Pennine and Maritime Alps, requires consideration.[43] His combination of normal medieval usage with the classical terms for the provinces of Tarentaise (Pennine Alps, actually Pennine and Graian Alps) and Embrun (Maritime Alps) is noteworthy. Perhaps Hugh knew some form of the *Notitia Galliarum,* a late antique administrative-geographical grid which remained popular into the Middle Ages.[44] Excepting Vienne, located within the Empire, and from which few prelates would have ventured to Alexander's council, all of the regions which he noted are represented in the new catalogue. But the total attendance which these districts contributed, according to Hugh, significantly exceeds—105 to 71 (including Béziers and Nîmes)—what the manuscript list offers for the same areas. This remains

so—98 to 77—even after the dioceses in the province of Vienne (7) are sub-
tracted from Hugh's figure and those in the manuscript list under Aix (6), a
province which Hugh omits (at least by name), are included in the manuscript's tally.[45]

Hugh's intention, in all likelihood, was to maximize the number of bishops
from the designated areas. This must have been accomplished simply by
adding the sees: before enumerating the provinces, he asserted that all of
the bishops from those regions came to the synod. Such a survey of dioceses in 1163, however, should have yielded 103, not 105.[46] This includes the
exempt bishopric of Le Puy and the province of Aix. Hugh does not mention the latter specifically, but it could have been subsumed either under
Narbonne—Aix was the metropolis of *Narbonensis secunda* in the *Notitia
Galliarum*[47]—or incorrectly, but from a geographical perspective, sensibly,
under Embrun.

An interesting correlation with Hugh's statistics emerges from the so-
called *provinciale* of Albinus, who died ca. 1196 as cardinal-bishop of Albano.[48] This compilation, partially based on the *Notitia* and frequently an
inaccurate guide to the ecclesiastical hierarchy of the twelfth century, is
preserved in Albinus's *Eglogarum digesta pauperis scholaris* (ca. 1189).[49]
It probably dates from earlier in the century, and has been attributed ten-
tatively to Cardinal Boso by the editors of the *Liber censuum*.[50] The number
of *civitates* registered there for the provinces under consideration, including
Aix, is 105. Did Hugh of Poitiers employ this work, conceivably produced
by none other than Boso, for his surmise about episcopal attendance?

Two supplements are possible to the new catalogue which help to fill the
gap between its 116 (or 118) bishops and Boso's 124. The first additions
concern Ireland, but are imprecise. Irish clergy were invited to the synod,[51]
and both Hugh of Poitiers and Romuald of Salerno said that some came.[52]
Their names are unavailable, but in all probability few risked the trip.
Glancing for comparison at the Scottish attendance, only a single bishop is
recorded, although possibly the abbot or his representative from the monastery of Dunfermline also took part.[53]

Twelfth-century journeys to Tours or Rome from frontier regions such as
Ireland and Scotland were arduous and costly.[54] Gerald of Wales testified
about the financial burden connected with attendance at such councils.
Writing a few decades after Tours, he described Bishop David of St. Davids'
intention to participate in that assembly.[55] The bishop sought and apparently received financial assistance for the trip from his clergy. His name,
however, does not appear in the manuscript census, either among the
Canterbury suffragans where he belongs (and where two Welsh sees do occur)
or elsewhere. The Cambrian dioceses mentioned are St. Asaph and Llandaff.
Bangor and St. Davids are missing, but the former was vacant in 1163.[56]

Bishop David is not one of the excused Canterbury suffragans noted by Ralph of Diceto, and he probably was on hand.[57] The present compilation may have omitted him, and the Irishmen with whom he could have traveled, because of absence (perhaps due to a late arrival) from the session where the bishops were catalogued.[58]

Nothing suggests that the series of names supplementing the Chichester *Annales* was anything but a private record. Whether it is based on an official document of the sort which William of Tyre made for the 1179 Lateran Council is unknown.[59] The text's author as well as its historical relation to the *Annales* are mysteries. If it was written by an eyewitness, rather than copied from another list, the compiler probably was in the delegation of Bishop Hilary of Chichester.[60]

Whoever the author was, his work does not betray an easily grasped order. Conciliar seating was not haphazard, and bishops were quite concerned about their places.[61] Roger Wendover stated that at the 1215 Lateran Council, "following the custom of general councils, individuals were positioned in their own rank."[62] Roger's remark is ambiguous; but in terms of bishops, it probably means that within a provincial delegation the suffragans were ranked according to seniority, that is when they were consecrated.[63] This formed a general but not irrevocable rule. At the Council of London in 1075, for example, in the face of procedural uncertainty, recourse was had to canonical authorities.[64] A series of venerable precedents advised that "individuals should be seated according to the time of their consecration, except for those who from ancient custom, or from the privileges of their churches, have preferred places."[65] After consultation with the oldest men present about "either what they had witnessed, or had learned as true from their elders," a general formula was devised. York would sit to the right and London to the left of Canterbury, with Winchester next to York. If the northern metropolitan was absent, London would be on the right and Winchester on the left. The other bishops should arrange themselves, on the basis of their consecration, around these prelates, probably in a semi-circle, horseshoe, or circle.[66]

A letter from Alexander III survives in which he commented on the seating at Tours, but not in as enlightening a way as could be hoped.[67] Writing to Archbishop Roger of York soon after the synod, the pontiff assured him that York's metropolitan privileges were not violated by what had happened therein. Alexander recalled that during the preliminaries, much bickering occurred among the English, and others as well, about seats. The episcopal chairs had not been arranged "according to the privileges which individuals claimed that they had from the papacy, and according to ancient and accustomed order." The latter phrase could mean according to consecration,

when no special papal privilege was applicable. Whether this refers to the
location of entire provincial contingents, or to the episcopal rank within
each province, or to both, is unclear. After considering the size of the cathedral ("short and narrow"), the pope had commanded orally that for the
present occasion regular order could be suspended. This was an ad hoc ruling, and was not to establish a precedent. Only at Tours could "anyone . . .
take and hold any place."

Whether or not arrangements were as chaotic as the pope depicts, traditional order, whatever it was, had been disrupted. Unfortunately, the new
list of bishops is useless for discovering how the assembly was constituted.
Consider the final four entries. The antepenultimate group is a collection of
exempt dioceses—León, Burgos, Le Puy, and Segni—under the heading *De
Hispania,* no doubt because of the first two.[68] This series is preceded by four
sees *De Lumbardia:* Milan, Pavia, Verona, and Turin. Milan was a metropolitan see with Turin as a suffragan; Pavia was immediately subject to
Rome; and Verona was in the province of Aquileia.[69] Following the bishop-
rics classed "From Spain" appears, *De Scotia,* Dunkeld, which belongs with
York.[70] The account ends with three bishops *De curia.*

The cardinals probably were seated on the papal dais at the head of the
assembly.[71] Were clerics from the exempt dioceses there too? If not on the
platform, they could have been somewhere else at the front of the council.
But then why did the compiler save them for the end of the catalogue? The
province of Tours surely had a choice place in the synod, and is listed first.
Answers to these questions can be only conjectural, but one such remark
might be permitted. Dieter Girgensohn has extracted a principle of geo-
graphical organization from the elaborate catalogue for the 1135 council at
Pisa.[72] The document associated with Tours could be analyzed similarly.
After the initial juxtaposing of Tours, Canterbury, Bourges, Bordeaux,
York, and Reims—a curious order perhaps explained by the confusion
Alexander described in his letter to York—a certain meandering through
France, then westward into Spain, then back eastward toward Italy, emerges
from the sequence Rouen, Sens, Lyons, Auch, Toledo, Compostela, Braga,
Tarragona, Narbonne, Aix, Embrun, Tarentaise, Lombardy, exempt sees,
and the curia. The problematic entry is Dunkeld, with its own heading
between the exempt dioceses and the cardinals—a perplexity to be treated
in the following chapter.

Within each province, also, there is little recognizable order. The two
bishops-elect, Dol and Worcester,[73] conclude the listings for the provinces of
Tours and Canterbury. The information provided by Gams and Pacaut,[74]
however, shows that the majority of delegations are not arranged according
to time of consecration, although Canterbury and Rouen do follow that

principle, with the adjustment of London in second place after Canterbury, according to the 1075 formula previously mentioned.[75] Whether the order in these two cases results more from what a Chichester man knew of Canterbury and Rouen than from what he saw in the council, and whether order could be imposed elsewhere if the provincial customs and special privileges were incorporated, is unknown. The first seems possible, the second unlikely given the suspension of canonical norms for the seating at Tours.

It remains to edit the text. In so doing the manuscript presentation has been altered as little as possible. Irregularities in the spelling of adjectival forms of place names have not been emended. Often the ending of such forms is indicated in the document only by a small "7" abbreviation sign, always above an *n*: *Redoneñ*, *Andegaveñ*, etc. Normally this sign would designate -*sis*: for example, *Redonensis*. In some cases, however, it probably represents -*ensis: Aureliañ* for *Aureliansis* is odd if not impossible, although *Aurelianus* seems to be possible.[76] The "7" sign is uncommon for -*us*, for which "9" is normal; that the compiler apparently employed both is suggested by *De provincia Compostellañ, ipse electus Compostellañ*. . . . The regular adjectival form of this place name follows the -*us*, -*a*, -*um* declension,[77] and it is bizarre if this was meant to read *De provincia Compostellanensi, ipse electus Compostellanus*. . . .[78] To permit such irregularities in the manuscript to be noted, all endings to adjectives designating places, supplied by expanding a "7," will be found in italics: Redonen*sis*. Capitalization and punctuation are editorial, and modern names are added in square brackets following each entry.

De provincia Turonensi [Tours], ipse archiepiscopus, et cum eo suffraganei eius videlicet Cenomannensis [Le Mans] episcopus, Redonen*sis* [Rennes], Andegaven*sis* [Angers], Nanneten*sis* [Nantes], Veneten*sis* [Vannes], Corisopiten*sis* [Quimper], Leonen*sis* [St.-Pol-de-Léon], Trecoren*sis* [Tréguier], Briocen*sis* [St.-Brieuc], Maclovien*sis* [St.-Malo], electus Dolen*sis* [Dol].

De provincia Cantuarien*si* [Canterbury], ipse archiepiscopus, et cum eo episcopi Lundonien*sis* [London], Elien*sis* [Ely], Salesberien*sis* [Salisbury], Norwicen*sis* [Norwich], Cicestren*sis* [Chichester], Rofen*sis* [Rochester], Exonien*sis* [Exeter], Coventren*sis* [Coventry-Lichfield], Landaven*sis* [Llandaff], episcopus de Sancto Asaf [St. Asaph], electus Wigorniensis [Worcester].

De provincia Bituricen*si* [Bourges], ipse archiepiscopus, et cum eo episcopi Claromonten*sis* [Clermont], Caturcen*sis* [Cahors], Rutinensis [Rodez], et Mimaten*sis* [Mende].

De provincia Burdegalensi [Bordeaux], ipse archiepiscopus, et cum eo episcopi Agenn*ensis* [Agen], Engolismensis [Angoulême], Xantonen*sis* [Saintes], Pictavien*sis* [Poitiers], Petragoricen*sis* [Périgueux].

De provincia Eboracensi [York], ipse archiepiscopus, et cum eo episcopus Dunelmensis [Durham].

De provincia Remensi [Reims], ipse archiepiscopus, et cum eo episcopi Suessionen*sis* [Soissons], Laudunen*sis* [Laon], Noviomen*sis* [Noyon], Tornacen*sis* [Tournai], Ambianen*sis* [Amiens], Morinen*sis* [Thérouanne], Belvacen*sis* [Beauvais], Silvanecten*sis* [Senlis].

De provincia Rotomagensi [Rouen], ipse archiepiscopus, et cum eo episcopi Ebroicensis [Évreux], Lexovien*sis* [Lisieux], Constantiensis [Coutances], Sagiensis [Séez], et Abrincensis [Avranches].

De provincia Senonensi [Sens], ipse archiepiscopus, et cum eo episcopi Carnoten*sis* [Chartres], Parisiacensis[79] [Paris], Aurelianen*sis* [Orléans], Autisiodoren*sis* [Auxerre], Nivernen*sis* [Nevers], Meldensis [Meaux], et Trecensis [Troyes].

De provincia Lugdun*ensi* [Lyons], episcopi Eduen*sis* [Autun], Lingonen*sis* [Langres], Matisconen*sis* [Mâcon], et Cabilonensis [Chalon-sur-Sâone].

De provincia Ausitanen*si* [Auch], episcopi Bigoritanus [Tarbes], Contienaren*sis* [Couserans],[80] Lasturren*sis* [Lescar], Aduren*sis* [Aire], Aquen*sis* [Dax], Baion*ensis* [Bayonne], Basaten*sis* [Bazas], et Lactoren*sis* [Lectoure].

De provincia Toletan*a*[81] [Toledo], ipse archiepiscopus, et cum eo episcopi Segobien*sis* [Segovia], et Seguntinen*sis* [Siguenza].

De provincia Compostellan*a* [Santiago de Compostela], ipse electus Compostellanus, et cum eo Avisen*sis* [Avila], et Caurien*sis* [Cória] episcopi.

De provincia Bracharen*si* [Braga], episcopi Lucen*sis* [Lugo], Asturicen*sis* [Astorga], et Zamorren*sis* [Zamora].[82]

De provincia Terragonen*si* [Tarragona], ipse archiepiscopus, et cum eo episcopi Calagoritanus [Calahorra], Pampilenen*sis* [Pamplona],[83] Titason*ensis* [Tarazona], Cesaraugustanus [Zaragoza], Ausonen*sis* [Vich], Dertusanus [Tortosa], Grunden*sis* [Gerona], Urgellen*sis* [Urgel], et Barchilonen*sis* [Barcelona].

De provincia Narbonensi [Narbonne], ipse archiepiscopus, et cum eo episcopi Carkasonen*sis* [Carcassonne], Agathen*sis* [Agde], Uteticen*sis* [Uzès], Magalonen*sis* [Maguelonne], Helenen*sis* [Elne], Lucdenen*sis* [Lodève], duo—Burrenen*sis* [Béziers],[84] Neumasen*sis* [Nîmes]—episcopi per nuntios.

De provincia Aquensi [Aix], ipse archiepiscopus, et cum eo episcopi Regensis [Riez], Foroiuliensis [Fréjus], Vapincen*sis* [Gap], et Abritensis [Apt].

De provincia Ebredunen*si* [Embrun], ipse archiepiscopus, et cum eo episcopi Antipolitanus [Antibes-Grasse], et Senecen*sis* [Sénez].

De provincia Tarentasiensi [Tarentaise], ipse archiepiscopus.

De Lumbardia [Lombardy], archiepiscopus Mediolanen*sis* [Milan], Papien-*sis* [Pavia], Veronen*sis* [Verona], et Taurinen*sis* [Turin] episcopi.

De Hispania [Spain], Legionen*sis* [León], Burgen*sis* [Burgos], Anitien*sis* [Le Puy] et Signinus [Segni][85] episcopi.

De Scotia [Scotland], Dunkeldenesis [Dunkeld] episcopus venit.

De curia, Hostiensis [Ostia], Portuensis [Porto], et Albanensis [Albano] episcopi.


## ABBOTS AND CARDINALS

Boso tabulated 414 abbots. But identifying them in primary sources, as opposed to speculating that so-and-so "must have been there," is nearly as problematic as trying to pick out individuals from that "great multitude of others, both clerics and laymen," which the cardinal also found at Tours.[86] The attendance lists, such as they are, for eleventh- and twelfth-century synods display little concern about abbots,[87] perhaps reflecting this group's subordination in council to the episcopacy.[88] The partial catalogue of those present at Clermont in 1095 lists only four abbots—and this document origi-nated in a monastic environment.[89] A compilation of the abbots at Tours would depend chiefly on two kinds of sources—papal letters and monastic records—but the rewards for pursuing this information are meager, in com-parison with the more than four hundred names being sought. A survey of papal letters dated in 1163 during and after the council has yielded only a single definite reference to an abbatial participant, Abbot Hugh of St.-Germain at Paris.[90] The participation of Abbot Geoffrey of St.-Bertin (at St.-Omer) emerges from the *Chronica* of that house by John *longus* de Ipra,[91] and undoubtedly combing other annals and similar texts would provide fur-ther names. The following can be noted from general sources for the synod: Matthew Paris testified to the presence of the abbots of St. Albans and of Bury St. Edmunds, but this account of their dispute at Tours is an excep-tional document; Hugh of Poitiers recorded the abbots of Cluny and Vézelay; and Robert of Torigny, from Mont St.-Michel, noted his own presence.[92]

A serious difficulty arises in using for this purpose the letters and monas-tic privileges obtained from Pope Alexander at Tours, during and following the council. Although such documents often were drafted expressly at the request of an abbot or prior, that petition was not always, and perhaps not even generally, made in person.[93] If an interview before the relevant papal officials is assumed, it need not have occurred in the council. A petititoner might appear, collect his document, and for whatever reasons then go home.[94] But many of the monasteries receiving papal letters during late May and early June 1163 obviously were represented in the synod, even if a list of those houses cannot serve as a guide to abbatial attendance. Although such a tabulation yields fewer than forty possibilities—a figure which falls short of Boso's by more than three hundred—and although not all of these religious establishments qualified for *abbatial* representation at the council, this information still is of interest. It provides, in the first place, an indication of the scope of Alexander's activities during the time of the assembly at Tours and shortly thereafter. Furthermore, to know some of the houses which sought and received documents from the pope, gives clues about his policy toward and his relations with the regular clergy at a crucial stage of his career.

The list which follows is derived from JL and the *Papsturkunden* volumes.[95] It includes letters which either are addressed to regular clerics or contain privileges for them, and which were issued between 19 May and 18 June 1163, that is from the opening of the synod to the time of Alexander's departure from Tours.[96] The purpose of this summary is simply to identify religious houses and orders, and no contextual synopses are attempted. These special sigla are used: C=Cottineau; KH=Knowles-Hadcock. For complete information and all other abbreviations, see the Bibliography.

| | |
|---|---|
| May 22 | Templars: JL 10860[97] |
| May 24 | Thornholme (Augustinian): KH 176; PUE 1.357, no. 95 |
| May 25 | St.-Jean at Amiens (Premonstratensian): C 1.85–86; JL 10861 |
| May 26 | Horsham St. Faith (Benedictine): KH 68; JL 10863 |
| | St.-Bertin (Benedictine): C 2.2615; JL 10864[98] |
| | St.-Loup at Troyes (Augustinian): C 2.3225; JL 10867 |
| | Snape (Benedictine): KH 76–77; JL 10868 |
| May 27 | Fountains (Cistercian): KH 119; PUE 3.286–87, no. 144 |
| May 28 | Christ Church, Canterbury (Benedictine): KH 61; PUE 2.298–99, no. 110 |
| | Colchester (Benedictine): KH 62–63; PUE 3.287–88, no. 145 |
| | St. Mary at Warwick (Secular college): KH 442; PUE 1.357–58, no. 96 |
| May 29 | St. Cuthbert at Durham (Benedictine): KH 64; PUE 2.299–300, no. 111 |
| May 31 | Sahagun (Benedictine, Cluniac): C 2.2574; JL 10870[99] |
| June 1 | Oseney (Augustinian): KH 169; PUE 3.288, no. 146 |
| | St.-Germain-des-Prés (Benedictine): C 2.2207; JL 10871 |
| June 2 | Hospitalers: JL 10872[100] |
| June 3 | Moutons (Benedictine nuns): C 2.2006; PUF 2.211–12, no. 118 |

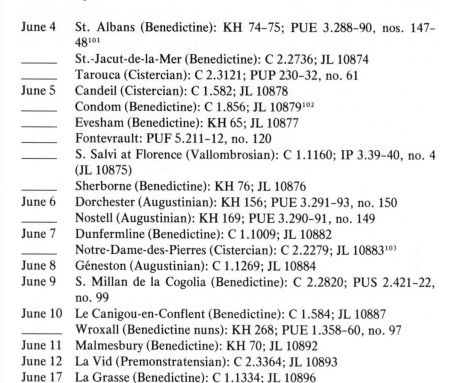

June 4    St. Albans (Benedictine): KH 74–75; PUE 3.288–90, nos. 147–48[101]

_____   St.-Jacut-de-la-Mer (Benedictine): C 2.2736; JL 10874

_____   Tarouca (Cistercian): C 2.3121; PUP 230–32, no. 61

June 5    Candeil (Cistercian): C 1.582; JL 10878

_____   Condom (Benedictine): C 1.856; JL 10879[102]

_____   Evesham (Benedictine): KH 65; JL 10877

_____   Fontevrault: PUF 5.211–12, no. 120

_____   S. Salvi at Florence (Vallombrosian): C 1.1160; IP 3.39–40, no. 4 (JL 10875)

_____   Sherborne (Benedictine): KH 76; JL 10876

June 6    Dorchester (Augustinian): KH 156; PUE 3.291–93, no. 150

_____   Nostell (Augustinian): KH 169; PUE 3.290–91, no. 149

June 7    Dunfermline (Benedictine): C 1.1009; JL 10882

_____   Notre-Dame-des-Pierres (Cistercian): C 2.2279; JL 10883[103]

June 8    Géneston (Augustinian): C 1.1269; JL 10884

June 9    S. Millan de la Cogolia (Benedictine): C 2.2820; PUS 2.421–22, no. 99

June 10   Le Canigou-en-Conflent (Benedictine): C 1.584; JL 10887

_____   Wroxall (Benedictine nuns): KH 268; PUE 1.358–60, no. 97

June 11   Malmesbury (Benedictine): KH 70; JL 10892

June 12   La Vid (Premonstratensian): C 2.3364; JL 10893

June 17   La Grasse (Benedictine): C 1.1334; JL 10896

The cardinals at Tours are easier to name than the abbots. Boso counted seventeen,[104] presumably including the cardinal-bishops. At the conclusion of the Chichester list, three cardinal-bishops are noted *De curia*—from Ostia, Porto, and Albano. Thirteen of the remaining fourteen can be named, with some probability, on the basis of the subscriptions to papal privileges dispatched at about the time of the council.[105] The following cardinals subscribed to documents issued proximate to May 19, the opening of the synod.[106] In each instance, only the occurrence closest to this date is given, for it is unknown how long the assembly lasted.[107] (Walter of Albano, Humbald of Ostia, and Bernard of Porto are frequent subscribers.)

JL 10859 (May 16):

    John, cardinal-priest of S. Anastasia

    Humbald, cardinal-priest of S. Croce in Gerusalemme

    Albert, cardinal-priest of S. Lorenzo in Lucina

    Henry, cardinal-priest of SS. Nereo e Achilleo

    Peter, cardinal-deacon of S. Eustachio iuxta Templum Agrippae

    Iacinthus, cardinal-deacon of S. Maria in Cosmedin

    Ardicius, cardinal-deacon of S. Teodoro
JL 10861 (May 25):
    John, cardinal-deacon of S. Maria in Porticu
JL 10863 (May 26):
    William, cardinal-priest of S. Pietro in Vincoli
    Odo, cardinal-deacon of S. Nicolao in Carcere Tulliano
PUF 2.213, no. 118 (June 3):
    Manfred, cardinal-deacon of S. Giorgio in Velabro
IP 3.39–40, no. 4 (JL 10875) (June 5):
    Cinthius, cardinal-deacon of S. Adriano
    Boso, cardinal-deacon of SS. Cosma e Damiano

This list, plus the three cardinal-bishops already named, accounts for six-teen of Boso's seventeen cardinals. The remaining prelate has escaped detection, although he must be one of the three others noted in JL as possible witnesses to papal bulls at this time[108]—Hildebrand, cardinal-priest of SS. XII Apostoli; John, cardinal-priest of SS. Giovanni e Paolo; or Raymond, cardinal-priest of S. Maria in Via lata.

# 4

## Conciliar Organization, III

SCOTLAND, YORK, AND CANTERBURY

Relations with York dominate the history of the Scottish Church during the twelfth century. The Scots' endeavor to escape the jurisdiction of an English metropolitan spanned many decades, coming to a successful end in 1192. In March of that year, Pope Celestine III issued the well-known bull beginning *Cum universi.*[1] The *ecclesia Scoticana,* defined by the dioceses of St. Andrews, Dunblane, Glasgow, Dunkeld, Brechin, Aberdeen, Moray, Ross, and Caithness, became a "special daughter" of the papacy, "subject to the apostolic see with no intermediary."

Alexander III's prominent role in this evolution has been marked by historians.[2] He has been termed a "consistent friend of the Scottish church and monarchy,"[3] despite obstacles now and then put in the way of this rapprochement, especially by King William "the Lion" of Scotland. A papal letter sent to William toward the end of Alexander's pontificate documents the capricious relations between these two leaders.[4] A schism at St. Andrews had produced tensions between pope and monarch.[5] Alexander reminded William how he had labored on behalf of him and his kingdom, and how much Scotland might suffer if the present strain continued.

This warning followed the events of the mid-1170s, which introduced "the most humiliating period of [William's] reign, the fifteen years of English overlordship."[6] The northern kingdom had become subject to Henry II, the conclusion of an ill-advised Scottish military campaign across the border in 1173. After his triumph, Henry moved to reintegrate the Church in Scotland firmly into the province of York.[7] The Scots had fought against this suffragan status on and off for at least fifty years, and now were supported unequivocally by the papacy.[8] Just when independence appeared close, however, King William clumsily intervened in an episcopal election at St.

33

Andrews, producing a local schism and the touchy situation evident in Alexander's letter.[9]

These developments are more than a decade subsequent to Tours. Is anything discernible relative to papal-Scottish relations in the 1163 council? Two factors can be examined: the participation of clerics from Scotland, and their seating in the assembly. On the basis of papal privileges dated about this time, Professor Barrow thought that Bishop Gregory of Dunkeld, and perhaps also Abbot Geoffrey of Dunfermline, were present.[10] Bishop Gregory's attendance is confirmed by the list edited in the previous chapter. No other Scots appear there, but, recalling the discussion about Irish and Welsh clergy,[11] this silence is not conclusive evidence.[12]

The last chapter speculated about a geographical progression—from northern France through Spain to Italy—for the sequence of middle and final delegations noted in the attendance catalogue (notwithstanding the insertion of Dunkeld near the end, between a group of exempt sees and the cardinals).[13] Was this a planned schema or only a coincidence? The answer is not at hand, but the compilation's first six, apparently unordered, provincial entries, together with Dunkeld's unexpected position, do permit one conjecture. Even if it is unclear where they were, the groups listed contiguously may have been proximate on the cathedral floor. The author might list together what he saw together, although where he was looking is unknown. The main difficulty here is that Tours comes first in the census and the cardinals last. The host province would be expected to have secured a choice place, despite Alexander's remarks about random seating,[14] but the cardinals would be so honored without question. A circular progression around the assembly could solve this. The author may have begun and ended his survey at the front, commencing with Tours, and concluding with the exempt and curial bishops, all of whom perhaps were on the papal dais.[15]

Gregory of Dunkeld could have been seated with this special group, a likelihood strengthened by Ralph of Diceto's testimony that he was not with York, where he would be expected: Archbishop Roger was accompanied only by a single suffragan, the bishop of Durham.[16] The bishop of Dunkeld's presence in a council apart from his nominal metropolitan is enigmatic. It could reflect the Scots' insistence that they were independent of York, and at most it might reveal the early stages of a Roman policy to support that attitude. The latter inference is obstructed, however, by Pope Alexander's assurance to Archbishop Roger that the seating at Tours had been according to expediency, that is the size of the church, and not according to ecclesiastical norms.[17] The pontiff had tolerated individuals occupying and retaining any spot, but this was not to create precedents. If Dunkeld was with the exempt dioceses, it probably was not a papal maneuver, and certainly not a forceful one. In all probability, either there simply was no place else to sit, or Bishop Gregory grasped at the relaxation of canonical procedures to exercise wishful thinking.

If space alone was the issue, that is if Gregory had been willing to sit with York provided there was room, it is improbable that Roger would not have squeezed an extra chair into his delegation. He was, at this time, especially sensitive about York's prerogatives, as the discussion of his bout with Canterbury will soon illustrate. If, on the other hand, Gregory had rebelled, Roger would have been forced to acquiesce, in view of Alexander's decision about seating. But the entire issue is complicated by what follows.

Tours provided another chapter in the lengthy quarrel between Canterbury and York about primacy in the English Church. The roots of this controversy, which still awaits a complete study, reach back to the time of Pope Gregory the Great; but the matter was pursued with urgency by Lanfranc, after his elevation to Canterbury following the Conquest.[18] Stephen of Rouen is the chief source for the incidents at Tours, although Alexander's post-conciliar letter to York is pertinent.[19] When poetic allowance has been made for the *Draco,* it is safe to say that Roger of York complained at Tours that he should have the first place among English participants: the province of York should be honored above Canterbury, since he had been consecrated before Thomas Becket. By 1163, the independence of these two ecclesiastical provinces had been confirmed by several twelfth-century popes, and Canterbury had suffered defeat in attempts to secure primacy over York.[20] As Alexander III wrote in January 1161, repeating earlier statements:

We forbid by apostolic authority that . . . the archbishop of Canterbury should demand from York, or that York should offer to Canterbury, any sort of profession . . . ; nor in any way should York be subject to the authority of Canterbury. But, according to the constitution [of St. Gregory], this honorific distinction should apply perpetually: whoever has been consecrated first takes precedence (*ut prior habeatur, qui prior fuerit ordinatus*).[21]

Roger was within his rights to demand precedence over Thomas in the council, and he seems to have carried on at length about it, raising the matter on different days.[22]

Despite what some historians have implied, this issue probably was not planned for the synodal agenda.[23] Henry II's disinclination for his prelates' carrying disputes beyond the realm, and Pope Alexander's compliance, at least for that time, weigh heavily against premeditation.[24] The archbishop of York must have raised the question in terms of conciliar procedure, and specifically in view of the seating arrangements. Exactly what annoyed him remains obscure, but the *Draco* and Alexander's letter permit the assumption that Canterbury either was assigned, or had arrogated for itself, a select place—a spot which Roger claimed in virtue of his seniority over Thomas

Becket. Aggressive on behalf of his see, Roger had gained from Alexander
by May 1163 several privileges, including that partially quoted above.[25] Professor Barlow's observation that York's devotion to Alexander during the
schism was in this way being rewarded, is consistent with the language of
those letters;[26] for example:

It is necessary to love in a special way those whom we recognize to be resolute (*promp-
tos*) and fervent above others in devotion to the sacrosanct Roman Church, and
consequently to honor them extraordinarily, so that they should not regret their
commitment to obedience and their devotion to the Church.[27]

Roger hardly would have been unaffected by the grand reception reportedly accorded to Thomas Becket on his arrival at Tours.[28] Such a display would
only heighten the tensions that had existed between these two men since
their days together under Archbishop Theobald.[29] Knowles has remarked
that "neither [Roger's] letters nor his recorded acts show the least trace of
any spiritual feeling."[30] It is, nonetheless, difficult to be unsympathetic to his
predicament in the council. He was only seeking what was his if papal prom-
ises were trustworthy.[31]

The *Draco* and Alexander do not specify whether Roger instigated formal
action to achieve his goal, but both his monarch's stand on such things and
the unique situation about the seating at Tours render it unlikely. He probably complained vigorously, and then tolerated less than he deserved. His
quandary resembles that faced by Abbot Robert of St. Albans in the same
gathering. Robert had lost the prime seat among the English abbots, which
*de iure* was his, through the machinations of Abbot Hugh of Bury St. Edmunds—another instance where seating was determined by possession and
not canon law.[32] Robert bemoaned his usurped dignity, but lodged no formal charge specifically because of Henry II's prohibition. Eventually, he
secured a place next to (*iuxta*) his rival, "above all the others."[33] The word
*iuxta* is imprecise here. Robert could either have resigned himself to the
second spot in the English monastic ranking, or somehow have wedged himself beside Hugh so that they shared the first position.

If compassion is needed for the archbishop of York at Tours, however,
it also is required for Pope Alexander. He had reached an understanding
with King Henry which permitted the English clergy to attend the synod,
but that very agreement precluded any action on disputed English affairs.
If the pope favored Canterbury in the seating confrontation, he would be
violating a series of papal privileges, including his own. But were he to support York, Alexander risked alienating the archbishop of Canterbury, whom
he probably deemed an indispensable contact between himself and the king,
notwithstanding the signs of strain appearing between Thomas and his monarch.[34] Either way, papal meddling in this "English" issue could irritate
Henry.

The episode is an instance in which Stephen of Rouen could have been much more helpful.[35] His distinctly partial account of Roger's offensive— "He placed himself before Thomas of Canterbury in every way, in words, ability (*ingenio*), prominence (*culmine*), primacy (*sede*), and seating (*loco*)"[36]—is followed by Alexander's response. The pope, as Stephen depicted him, was overwhelmed by the vigor of Roger's performance; but, like any good politician resolving a dispute, he set forth his decision as a compromise. The two English delegations were separated. Perhaps intending to show York in the best light vis-à-vis Canterbury, the *Draco* noted that subsequently they occupied equally honorific positions in different parts of the church. According to Ralph of Diceto, Thomas sat to the right with his suffragans, and Roger, with only the bishop of Durham, "was ordered" (*jussus est*) to sit on the left.[37] Right and left of what is unstated, but presumably the papal throne at the front of the assembly provided orientation.[38]

It is too fanciful, in all likelihood, to read into Ralph's remarks the traditionally pejorative context of "sinister" things. If he was correct, however, and York had been "ordered" to a particular place, Canterbury retained the disputed spot. The compromise became a victory for Archbishop Thomas. Since Pope Alexander felt obligated after the council to assert that the seating had not damaged York's prerogatives, it appears that wherever Roger finally settled, his rival was better situated.[39] Notwithstanding political considerations, Thomas Becket's personality might have influenced the Roman pontiff's decision. The shrewd Italian diplomat and the former Anglo-Norman chancellor, of "commanding presence," who "never misjudged men,"[40] must have impressed each other favorably. William of Newburgh reported a rumor that Thomas secretly resigned his archiepiscopal see at Tours, because he had received it *minus sincere et canonice,* and then was reinstated by Alexander.[41]

However the meager evidence is interpreted, the pope's suspension of regular procedures for conciliar seating was justified by a reference to the dimensions of the church. Whether that be truth or rationalization, it was not an unreasonable way to explain what had happened. Canterbury's suffragan contingent was much larger than York's. It would entail greater confusion to move the former than to relocate York and Durham. Perhaps just when Alexander ordered those two delegations to another area, Gregory of Dunkeld slipped away to secure a seat with or beside the exempt churches. In a crowded assembly, amid the turmoil of synodal preliminaries, such an escape might have succeeded for many reasons, even if his archbishop had protested. At that moment, however, would Roger have troubled himself about an obscure Scottish see? He may have been too preoccupied, for he had just lost to his chief adversary a battle that should have been no contest.

Alexander's apology to Roger after the council reiterated the definition of honorific preeminence in terms of seniority.[42] The facts at Tours had been otherwise. Stephen of Rouen wrote as follows of the final Canterbury-York configuration: "Equals in sees [or "in seats"—*sedibus*], they are equals in honor."[43] For York at that time, however, honorific equality was a defeat. Whether by architectural or papal design, Roger was forced to be "equal," and thus compelled to tolerate less than that *prior habeatur, qui prior fuerit ordinatus.*

Subsequent history is an unreliable guide to the issues between Scotland, York, and Canterbury in May 1163, for the great controversy which exploded in England soon thereafter colored relations between Rome and Britain for the following decade. But by the mid-1170s, after the military defeat of William the Lion but before the St. Andrews schism, Pope Alexander sympathized openly and deeply with the Scottish Church. In July 1176, he wrote to the bishops in Scotland thus:

It troubles us that our dearest son in Christ, the illustrious King Henry of England, has compelled you to swear to obey the English Church, since this implies an injury to God and contempt for us, as well as contempt for ecclesiastical liberty. . . . We, however, unwilling to tolerate that your liberty should be diminished, have firmly commanded our venerable brother the archbishop of York, legate of the apostolic see, that he should not exercise metropolitan jurisdiction, until by means of an examination by the Roman pontiff, it becomes known whether you ought to be subject to him by metropolitan law.[44]

At the Lateran Council in 1179, according to the extant but incomplete attendance lists, the Scottish delegation formed a separate entity, and was not part of the York province.[45] Only Bishop Gregory of Ross is named under the heading *Provincia Scotiae,* but two other Scottish prelates were consecrated by Pope Alexander at the synod, probably the bishops of Brechin and Dunblane.[46] The papal declaration just quoted makes it clear why the Scots did not sit as suffragans of York in 1179. Gregory of Dunkeld's actions in 1163 are less transparent, and more intriguing.

# 5

---

# The Conciliar Canons

This chapter discusses both the survival of the canons from Tours and their content. The object of the "Transmission" section is to indicate the genuine decrees, how they are preserved, and what is required before they can be edited critically. A new edition is less urgent for Tours than for other synods (see the Preface), but the 1163 texts do raise certain important problems which entail the use of special terms and methods. Although an effort has been made to define and elucidate these technicalities when they arise, this portion of the chapter is divided, and the middle two sections could be skimmed by those interested in a non-technical approach to the subject.

## TRANSMISSION

### I

The authentic canons from the synod at Tours survive in at least three ways. Nine of them are in Cardinal Boso's *Vita Alexandri*.[1] The first eight of these occur, in a different order, in William of Newburgh.[2] The same eight plus another possibly genuine item, which is given by neither Boso nor William (the so-called "c. 10," discussed in section IV below), survive variously in books called decretal collections assembled between the last years of Alexander III and 1234.[3] The synod is, therefore, the recognized source for nine or ten canons.

The additional dozen "Tours" canons in Mansi, taken from Martène and Durand's *Thesaurus,* are spurious, wrongly attributed as a result of confusion in some decretal collections.[4] The ninth item in the published sequence of this inauthentic set occurs, also ascribed to the 1163 assembly, in the *Decretales* of Pope Gregory IX (5.37.4). It was noticed there long before

39

Martène-Durand's time by Cardinal Baronius.[5] His observation was repeated at least twice in seventeenth-century conciliar works—by Binius, and in the French *Collectio regia* in 1644[6]—and then dropped, properly but for no stated reason, in Labbe-Cossart's *Sacrosancta concilia* of 1671–72.[7]

Aside from Boso's final canon, bearing chiefly on the schism, and "c. 10," peculiar to the decretal tradition, Boso, William, and the canonical compilations transmit the same eight decrees. The interrelation of these texts, and their ultimate source(s), remain undetermined. As mentioned earlier, Boso's account of the synod must be regarded highly.[8] The decretal collectors, on the other hand, also could have possessed authoritative versions from papal circles, either directly or through copies.[9]

William's presentation probably emanated from either a decretal collection or a report transmitted by one of the council's English participants. Early modern scholars knew the canons in the *Historia rerum Anglicarum,* and noted also that their order differed from those in the *Vita Alexandri* (William's series=Boso's cc. 5, 6, 7, 1, 2, 4, 3, 8). Binius, in effect, used William to authenticate some of the same texts found ascribed to Tours in the decretal collection known as the *Appendix* (to the Third Lateran Council).[10] Such reliance on William probably can be explained by the manuscript tradition of the *Vita.*

Only toward the end of the last century was Boso recognized as the author of that unsigned life of Alexander.[11] How this series of papal lives, some of which he composed, some of which he merely edited, was transmitted during and soon after Boso's lifetime is unknown. From the middle of the thirteenth century, the set occurred as a supplement to the *Liber censuum* (LC). The rationale for such an amalgamation can only be guessed, but the insertion exists in the earliest surviving copy of the original late twelfth-century LC (where the lives are not found). This transcript, now in the Biblioteca Riccardiana at Florence (MS 228), was an official chancery replacement for the original. All later known copies of LC, whether containing or omitting the *vitae,* stem from this *codex Riccardianus.* One such derivative was an amplification of LC prepared in the fourteenth century by Cardinal Nicholas Roselli. Roselli incorporated the papal lives virtually unchanged, and Baronius occasionally cited them according to this source.[12] But the twelfth-century origins of the compilation were by now obscure, and hence Binius, in the seventeenth century, could consider William of Newburgh's list of the decrees to be a better, or at least an earlier, witness.

Louis Duchesne's edition of Boso ignored all manuscripts other than the mid-thirteenth-century Riccardian codex.[13] That edition serves as the most reliable printed source for the *Vita*'s canons, if only because its genealogy is apparent. To an overwhelming degree of probability, all of the conciliar

editions, Binius (following Baronius) to Mansi, reproduced a version derivative in some way from that same manuscript.[14] Speculation about their
actual copies is unnecessary here. It is noteworthy, however, that Boso's
decrees underwent two editions between Baronius and Mansi. The text of
the former was taken over by Binius, and from there was included in the
*Collectio regia* of 1644. Labbe-Cossart prepared a new edition, which passed
through Hardouin and Coleti to Mansi.[15]

Despite the early modern editors' usual reticence about manuscripts, a
tantalizing nugget of information comes from Baronius. In addition to their
presence in the *Vita Alexandri,* the decrees from Tours were noticed "in a
manuscript of ancient canons in the Vatican Library" (*in codice antiquorum
canonum in Vaticana bibliotheca*);[16] and Baronius's published edition of the
canons is accompanied by marginal variants labelled *Vat.* A source so designated could hardly be another copy of Boso via LC, and the reference must
denote a canonical collection and probably a decretal compilation. Nothing
further can be asserted beyond the hope that reading at other points in the
*Annales ecclesiastici,* or investigation of Baronius's unpublished notes (preserved in Rome at the Biblioteca Vallicelliana), might uncover this codex.

## II

The first chapter fixed attention briefly on the institutional growth of the
Church in the twelfth century.[17] The importance in that development of the
papal decretal letter engendered a "remarkably vigorous and creative school
of decretal compilators in and after the closing decade of Alexander III's
pontificate."[18] The books produced by such editors contained, for the most
part, recent papal documents, both letters and conciliar rulings. In the latter category, Alexander's synods at the Lateran in 1179 and at Tours are
especially prevalent.

The history of decretal collections remains to be written. It can be observed generally that toward the end of Pope Alexander's reign, mere textual accumulations (primitive collections) were giving way to sophisticated
compendia (systematic collections), in which canons were shorn of all legally
extraneous material and distributed into several books under specific head-
ings. The appearance ca. 1191 of Bernard of Pavia's *Breviarium* (*Comp. I*)—
the first of the so-called *Quinque compilationes antiquae* (*antiqua*=pre-
Gregorian *Decretales;* see below)—established a schema which "became the
model for all later collections of any distinction."[19] Bernard's work was in
five books, each possessing a separate heading, subdivided into titles under
which the canons were arrayed. *Comp. I* thus provided a format, and the
*Quinque compilationes* (QCA) contributed the bulk of the texts, for the volu-
minous *Liber extravagantium decretalium* promulgated in 1234 by Pope

Gregory IX.[20] This was an official work, offering an authoritative selection
of canonical material from the age of the *ius novum,* that is dated after the
appearance of Gratian's *Decretum.*

As mentioned already, scholars such as Baronius and Binius recognized
that decretal compilations preserved texts imputed to Tours.[21] Binius spoke
of eight such canons, "which . . . are contained . . . in the *Appendix* of the
eleventh ecumenical council (which had assembled) at the Lateran."[22] That
reference designates an important systematic decretal collection—the so-
called *Appendix concilii Lateranensis* (Lateran III, 1179), which was noted
fleetingly above.[23] The title is misleading, for the work is independent of
that synod, composed perhaps in Italy but more likely in England, in the
1180s.[24] Of the eight texts which Binius found therein, six probably are
authentic.[25] Five certainly are, repeating Boso's cc. 1, 2, 5, 6 and 8; the sixth
is the "c. 10" mentioned at the outset of this chapter, which will be treated
below in section IV. *Appendix* also includes Boso's cc. 3 and 7, but without
proper inscriptions.[26] Labbe-Cossart had observed that the seven canons
from the *Vita Alexandri* in this compilation, plus one more (c. 4), are scat-
tered among various titles in *Comp. I,* and a single canon (c. 3) appears in
*Comp. II* (assembled 1210–15).[27] From these two works all but c. 4 passed
into the *Decretales* of Gregory IX.

The following table illustrates the distribution of the 1163 legislation in
*Appendix* (by title and canon), in QCA (book, title, and canon), and in the
1234 *Decretales* (X) (book, title, and canon). The numbers for the canons in
the first column are those of the *Vita Alexandri.*

|   | *App.* | QCA | X |
|---|---|---|---|
| 1 | 30.4 | I 3.5.10 | 3.5.8 |
| 2 | 16.9 | I 5.15.1 | 5.19.1 |
| 3[28] | 26.8 | II 3.17.2 | 3.30.17 |
| 4 | ____ | I 5.6.10 | ____ |
| 5 | 2.2 | I 5.3.3 | 5.4.3 |
| 6 | 2.10 | I 5.2.7 | 5.3.8 |
| 7 | 2.1 | I 5.3.2 | 5.4.2 |
| 8 | 27.2 | I 3.37.2 | 3.50.3 |

These certainly are not the only systematic collections into which Tours
enters, as even the incomplete apparatus to Friedberg's edition of X will illustrate readily.[29] It is necessary also to remember the evolving practice of
"ruthless elimination," in the systematic collections especially, aimed at
presenting only the legally important segment of a text.[30] By using italics
and various symbols, Friedberg has attempted to indicate how decrees were
trimmed as they passed through QCA into the Gregorian collection. The

canons from Tours which enter the 1234 promulgation are only excerpts of what Alexander III had decreed seven decades earlier.

### III

The remarks given so far about decretal compilations are historiographical—a listing of the canons from the assembly at Tours in three collections where earlier writers had recognized them. Before a modern edition is possible, the occurrences of these decrees must be investigated throughout the decretal corpus. The results will aid in untangling what can be termed, pending that further investigation, the "canonical" and the "literary" traditions: the decretal transmission, and Boso and William of Newburgh.

The strength of the "canonical" tradition, and its claim to at least an equal centrality with Boso, are demonstrated by the presence of canons from Tours in several additional twelfth-century decretal collections. As a result of his extensive study of these works, the late Walther Holtzmann published several annotated lists of the known compilations. The most recent was issued at the beginning of the "Kanonistische Ergänzungen" (1957) to the *Italia pontificia*. The collections registered there are designated generally as primitive or systematic, and arranged geographically in a chronological schema.[31] Although at points subject to revision,[32] this tabulation provides a useful census. The systematic compilations offer a "dismemberment of the individual decretals" among titles,[33] and are less appropriate than the primitive collections in an analysis of how any bloc of texts penetrated into the literature. For the present sampling, therefore, with one omission,[34] primitive collections dated by Holtzmann prior to *Comp. I* (1191), where at least five canons appear consecutively or nearly so, have been admitted.[35] Details about the collections will not be given, since they are available readily in Holtzmann's lists, in Duggan, *Collections,* or in Kuttner, *Repertorium.* All probably date between the mid-1170s and 1191, and most in the years immediately after the 1179 Lateran Council. The general classification and the details of manuscripts are repeated from Holtzmann's latest survey, and the enumeration of the canons follows Boso. Furthermore, no note will be made in these tabulations of the few instances where canons are run together, without distinct divisions.

FRENCH GROUP

*Coll. Parisiensis I:* Paris, Bibliothèque nat. MS lat. 1596, fols. 26v–28r, cc. 4, 5, 6, 7, 8, 2: see Friedberg, CS 57.[36]

ITALIAN GROUP[37]

*Coll. Ambrosiana:* Milan, Biblioteca del capitolo di S. Ambrogio MS M57, fol. 311r–v, cc. 5, 6, 7, 8, JL 14055, cc. 4, 1, 2, 3.

*Coll. Floriana:*[38] St. Florian, Stiftsbibl. MS III. 5, fol. 175r-v, cc. 3, 4, 8, 5, 6, 7, 1, 2.

*Coll. Cusana:* Cues, Hospitalbibl. MS 229, fols. 93r-94r, cc. 5, 6, 7, 8, 4, 1, 2, 3.

*Coll. Berolinensis I:* Berlin, Deutsche Staatsbibl. MS Phill. 1742, fol. 292r, cc. 5, 6, 7, 8, 4, 1, 2, 3: see Juncker, 383-85.

ENGLISH GROUP

*Coll. Belverensis:* Oxford, Bodleian MS e Mus. 249, fols. 121r-122r, cc. 5, 6, 7, 8, 3, 1, 2, 4: see Duggan, *Collections* 155; Brooke, 480; and Brooke-Morey-Brooke, xlii, 1, and 3.

*Coll. Dunelmensis III:* Durham, Cathedral Library MS C.III.1, fol. 14r-v, cc. 5, 6, 7, 8, 4, 1, 2, 3: see Kuttner, "Biberach" 71, Additional note.

*Coll. Fontanensis:* Oxford, Bodleian MS Laud Misc. 527, fols. 43v-44r, cc. 4, 5, 6, 7, 8, JL 12020, 3: see Brooke, 480.

BRIDLINGTON GROUP

*Coll. Bridlingtonensis:* Oxford, Bodleian MS Bodl. 357, fols. 132r-133v, cc. 5, 6, 7, 8, 4, 1, 2, 3: see Duggan, *Collections* 93.

*Coll. Claudiana:* London, British Library MS Cotton Claud. A IV, fol. 191r-v, cc. 8, 5, 6, 7, 3, 1, 2: see Duggan, *Collections* 90.

In addition to this information from decretal collections which have been registered by Holtzmann, the following *varia* can be reported.

1. Biberach an der Riss, Spitalarchiv MS B.3515, twelfth-century *Decretum Gratiani,* with supplements; fol. 237r-v, cc. 5, 6, 7, 4, 8, 3, 2, 1: see Weigand, "Biberach" 79; Kuttner, "Biberach" 67 and 71, Additional note.

2. Durham, Cathedral Library MS B.IV.17, twelfth-century Burchard of Worms, *Decretum,* with supplements; fols. 172v-173r, cc. 5, 6, 7, 8, 4, 1, 2, 3:[39] see R. A. B. Mynors, *Durham Cathedral Manuscripts to the End of the Twelfth Century* (Oxford 1939) 67.

3. Montecassino, Biblioteca dell' Abbazia MS 64, twelfth-century *Decretum Gratiani,* with supplements; p. 537, cc. 5, 6, 7, 8, 4, 1, 2, 3: see Kuttner, *Repertorium* 48 and 274-75.

4. Paris, Bibliothèque nat. MS lat. 2259, twelfth/thirteenth-century Gregory I, *Homilies,* with supplements; fol. 123v, cc. 5, 6, 7, 8, 3, 1, 2, 4: see P. Lauer, *Catalogue général des manuscrits latins,* 2 (Paris 1940) 377.

5. _____, MS lat. 2472, twelfth-century Ivo of Chartres, *Panormia,* with supplements; fol. 107, cc. 5, 6, 7?, 8, 1, 2, 3, 4: see Kuttner, "Notes" 536-37.

6. _____, MS lat. 15001, probably twelfth-century, canonical *varia*; fols. 237r–238r, cc. 5, 6, 7, 8, 3, 1, 2, 4: see Kuttner, "Biberach" 67, and *Repertorium* 263 and 286–87.

A glance at these two sets of information reveals an unexpected variety in the order of the canons. Out of sixteen occurrences, no arrangement appears more than seven times (5, 6, 7, 8, 4, 1, 2, 3). Furthermore, and perhaps more surprising, none of the series repeats either Boso or William of Newburgh (5, 6, 7, 1, 2, 4, 3, 8). The only discernible trend in terms of Holtzmann's geographical distribution is that the most common sequence predominates in the Italian group. One clear fact is that cc. 5, 6, and 7 form a constant series. In the present sampling, plus William, they always are together, in that order, and in the majority of instances they come at or very near the beginning of the group. They constitute a stable core around which the other canons are variously disposed.

IV

Resolution of this numerical jumble will involve searching for new manuscript evidence, collations, and comparison of inscriptions and divisions within and between the canons. But the puzzles offered by the 1163 legislation are not compassed by the texts common to Boso, William, and the decretal compilers. Attention must also be given to what might be termed a maverick canon, transmitted solely in the canonical sources. The text is lengthy, nearly four times longer than any of the other nine. It first appeared as part of the conciliar editors' presentation for the assembly at Tours in Labbe-Cossart, as c. 10, following directly the nine items from the *Vita Alexandri*.[40] The source is not mentioned, but marginal references are offered to *Appendix* (title 31, c. 6), and to *Comp. II* (book 3, title 27, c. 1), and the text may have been printed from some version of one of these. In both, the inscription is unambiguous: *Idem in Turonensi concilio,* and *Turon. conc. sub Alexandro III celebratum,* respectively.[41]

*Appendix* is not free of counterfeit canons from the assembly at Tours, and a misattribution here is possible.[42] *Appendix* and *Comp. II* are not, however, the only decretal collections where "c. 10" appears. These two works are, in fact, chronological boundaries for a series of compilations which include it. The following list, as nearly as possible in chronological order, and formulated mainly from printed literature, shows where the canon has been observed.

1. *Appendix* (ca. 1181–85): title 31, c. 6: printed in Crabbe, 907; Mansi, 22. 385–87 (see note 23 above, for relevant remarks).
2. *Coll. Tanneri* (ca. 1187–91): Oxford, Bodleian MS Tanner 8, fol. 591r: see Holtzmann, "Tanner" 105.

3. *Coll. Cheltenhamensis* (1181-ca. 1193): London, British Library MS Egerton 2819, fols. 21v–22r: see Duggan, *Collections* 103.

4. *Coll. Cottoniana* (ca. 1193–94): London, British Library MS Cotton Vitellius E XIII, fol. 204r–v: see Duggan, *Collections* 107.[43]

5. *Coll. Peterhusensis* (ca. 1194): Cambridge, Peterhouse MS 193, fol. 222r: see Brooke, 480.[44]

6. *Coll. Sangermanensis* (ca. 1198): Paris, Bibliothèque nat. MS lat. 12459, fol. 1r: see Singer, 68–70 and 117; Brooke, 480.

7. *Coll. Abrincensis* (soon after *Sang.*): Avranches, Bibliothèque mun. MS 149, fol. 79r–v: see Singer, 77 and 355.

8. *Coll. Lucensis* (ca. 1199): Lucca, Biblioteca cap. MS 221, fols. 225v–226r: see Heyer, "Singer, *Dekretalensammlung*" 588; Kuttner, "Notes-Decretal Letters" 350.

9. *Coll. Halensis* (ca. 1201): Halle, Universitäts- und Landesbibl. MS Ye.80, fols. 88v–89v: see Heyer, "Singer, *Dekretalensammlung*" 591.

10. *Coll. Alani* (ca. 1206): (for manuscripts see the references given), book 3, title 24, c. 3: see von Heckel, 281; Kuttner, "Alanus" 41.

(11. *Coll. Estensis* [soon after *Coll. Alani*]: Modena, Biblioteca Esten. MS α R.4, 16, fol. 104r–v: see Kuttner, "Notes-Decretal Letters" 351; Holtzmann, KE 65. This collection is derivative from Alanus and also from the *Coll. Gilberti,* where the relevant canon does not occur. The parentheses indicate that the transmission seems certain. The same transmission holds also for the following occurrence.)

(12. *Coll. Fuldensis* [soon after *Coll. Alani*]: Fulda, Landesbibl. MS D.3a, fol. ?? [*Coll. Fulden.* =entire manuscript), book 3, title 31, c. 4: see von Heckel, 337.)

13. *Comp. II* (1210-15): (for manuscripts see Kuttner, *Repertorium* 345ff.), book 3, title 27, c. 1: see Friedberg, QCA 90–91.

An involved discussion of this decree's transmission is premature, on the basis of a list assembled chiefly from secondary literature, but a few tentative observations can be offered. Alanus is a well-known source of *Comp. II.*[45] The identical inscriptions for "c. 10" in both places—*Turon. concilium sub Alexandro III celebratum*[46]—makes *Comp. II*'s direct debt to that canonist likely in this instance. Once that has been said, other generalizations become more involved and more tenuous. The *Coll. Lucensis* and *Halensis,* for example, await detailed study. An eighteenth-century edition of the former by Mansi printed the following fragmentary inscription for "c. 10": *Incipit . . . Turon. sub Alexandro III.*[47] Early in this century, in a series of remarks on these two works, Friedrich Heyer commented on their authors' use of papal registers,[48] but no specific allusion was made to the decree under consideration.[49]

The *Coll. Abrincensis,* using primarily *Coll. Sangermanensis,* intended
to supplement *Comp. I.*[50] But *Sang.* was not the sole source for *Abrin.* In
both works, the texts from Tours are located at the beginning. Each collection opens this series with "c. 10," followed by other texts, both genuine and
spurious, attributed to the same synod. *Abrin.*'s sequence, however, includes
material absent from *Sang.*[51] Furthermore, although this alone would be of
less significance, the latter's distinctive attribution—*Concilium Turonense
celebratum sub Alexandro papa III*—is reduced in *Abrin.* simply to *Concilium Turonense.* Thus the facile solution about the transmission of "c. 10"
between these books is difficult. *Abrin.* received some decrees attributed to
the council in 1163, and perhaps the entire set used in the collection, from
somewhere other than *Sang.*

According to Holtzmann, *Sang.* employed three sources: *Comp. I,* the
*Coll. Brugensis,* and the *Coll. Tanneri.*[52] Of these, the relevant canon appears only in *Tann.* There is, in fact, great similarity between the sequence
of canons imputed to Tours in the St.-Germain and Tanner compilations.[53]
Professor C. N. L. Brooke, discussing conciliar statutes in early decretal
works, reduced Holtzmann's assertion by noting that "the immediate source
of the *Sangermanensis* was a collection similar to the *Collectio Tanner.*"[54]
*Tann.* itself is, nonetheless, a reasonable spot to hunt *Sang.*'s source for
"c. 10," despite the former's inscription—*Incipit concilium Turonense*—
resembling more closely the attribution in *Abrin.* than the inscription in
*Sang.* In addition, *Tann.,* and/or *Sang.,* may have been used by Alanus:[55]
comparing inscriptions, for the present case, the latter would appear more
likely. But detailed collations are required before a transmission could be
constructed backward from Alanus, and, therefore, in all likelihood, from
*Comp. II,* through *Sang.* (or *Abrin.*?), to *Tann.*

Professor Brooke wrote that *Tann.* "is a copy of the *Collectio Bamber-
gensis* with additional material from a text of the Worcester group inserted."[56] The latter is a large family of decretal collections, so designated
because the *Coll. Wigorniensis* once had been considered the oldest extant
member.[57] The *Coll. Bamb.,* one of "the most common systematic collection[s] of decretals before Compilatio I,"[58] has been studied in detail. The re-
puted tenth decree from Tours is missing there, and in all members of the
so-called Bamberg group.[59] The Worcester family, on the other hand, of
which the *Coll. Cheltenhamensis, Cottoniana,* and *Peterhusensis* are developed members, has not been analyzed thoroughly.[60] Neither of two early
components—the *Coll. Wigorn.,* and the *Coll. Claustroneoburgensis*—has
"c. 10,"[61] but *Chelt., Cott.,* and *Peterhus.* do, with *Peterhus.* displaying
an arrangement of authentic 1163 material mixed with spurious items similar to *Tann.* and especially *Sang.*[62]

The relevant text's presence in *Appendix,* and in *Coll. Lucensis* and *Halensis,* removes the easy solution of relegating it to the Tours *spuria* permeating several Anglo-Norman compilations in the final quarter of the twelfth century. Although, as noted, *Appendix* is not free from counterfeits,[63] it is not the main line by which faulty "Tours" items infiltrated the decretal literature.[64] No immediate interdependence existed between *Coll. Wigorn.* and *Appendix.*[65] Whether *Appendix,* either directly or indirectly, furnished the route for the assumption of this decree into the developed members of the Worcester family remains, for the present, unknown.

V

As a supplement to the printed edition of Boso's canons from Tours, Mansi provided variant readings from a manuscript "which once was in the possession of His Eminence Cardinal Passionei, written, as I suspect, in the thirteenth century."[66] Mansi's notes designate specific alternative readings for the preface to the decrees, and for cc. 3, 4, and 6, adding, finally, that "the remainder are read as they are emended here in the margin, by Labbe." The decrees printed are accompanied by the marginal apparatus appearing first in Labbe-Cossart,[67] which offers variants, after c. 6, for cc. 7 and 8.

To this point, Mansi has implied the discovery of a reproduction of the nine canons, in what he assumed to be a thirteenth-century copy. If the dating were correct, that text would constitute an early witness for the decrees, but the codex in question, in all likelihood, would be a version of the *Liber censuum* based on MS Riccardianus 228.[68] The editor's final statement on the matter, however, dispels routine hypotheses. After marking the equivalence of his variants to Labbe's, for the items after c. 6, he concluded by writing that "the others, following c. 10, are not read in [the?] manuscript" (*Reliqua vero post canonem X. in Cod. non leguntur*). The "others" so designated are the aforementioned spurious canons taken from Martène-Durand.[69] Those texts are printed in Mansi, immediately following the ten decrees composed of the nine from the *Vita Alexandri* plus "c. 10." Mansi is asserting that the *spuria* were not read in his collated manuscript, but that the tenth canon was.

Ingenuity could be expended to show why Mansi did not mean what he said. Perhaps *post canonem X* is a mistake, maybe a printer's error, for *post canonem IX.* Or, since he did see "c. 10" in the *Coll. Lucensis,*[70] his observation might be stretched to imply two codices. He had not seen the items after "c. 10" in any manuscript, although the capital "C" on *Cod.* makes the general translation "in manuscript" problematic. The best resolution would be to retrieve the book that Mansi used.

It once had belonged to Cardinal Domenico Passionei (d. 1761), an important eighteenth-century ecclesiastical statesman, and one of the great bibliophiles of his age.[71] He was named prefect of the Vatican Library in 1755 by Pope Benedict XIV, and his private library comprised 40,000 volumes. After Passionei's death, most of this collection passed to the Augustinians, and later was added to the Biblioteca Angelica in Rome.[72] About 6,000 volumes had a different fate, however, becoming the nucleus of the Biblioteca civica in Fossombrone (Passionei's birthplace), while a few others ultimately went to the Vatican.[73] Somewhere in this mélange, the book from which Mansi extracted his variants probably still exists.

VI

The previous discussions have indicated several points of uncertainty about the transmission of the 1163 decrees.[74] The search for Baronius's *codex antiquorum canonum,* and Mansi's Passionei manuscript, could yield surprising results; but it seems unlikely that further investigation of Boso or William of Newburgh would offer much. The major area for additional study, the possibility of new discoveries aside, centers on the decretal collections. The presence and transmission of the legislation from the synod at Tours in these works requires systematic analysis, and ultimate correlation with Boso and William. Such work would supersede what has been sketched here, would establish a firm basis for evaluating the claims of "c. 10," and ultimately would lead to a critical edition of all nine or ten authentic decrees.

CONTENT

The following discussion is based on the canons from the Council of Tours as edited by Duchesne in Boso's life of Alexander III, and for "c. 10" by Friedberg in QCA. It begins with a summary of the texts, adhering to the Latin statements as closely as possible. In parentheses following each is the title under which the provision occurs in the relevant section of QCA and the 1234 Gregorian *Decretales* (X); these titles show how the decrees were viewed thematically by canonists in the twelfth and thirteenth centuries. (For the precise locus of each item in QCA and X, see page 42 above).

1. Division of benefices and alteration of "dignities" (church offices) prohibited. (*Comp. I:* Concerning prebends [*De prebendis*]; X: Concerning prebends and dignities [*De prebendis et dignitatibus*]).
2. Prohibition of clerical usury, and, in particular, condemnation of clerics who have received a mortgage from debtors and then retain earnings from this property which are not applied toward liquidation of the loan. An exception is made in the case of an ecclesiastical benefice held by a layman and offered as a pledge, which in this way could be repurchased from lay hands. (*Comp. I:* Concerning usury [*De usuris*]; X: same)

3. Churches, tithes, and oblations are not to be granted to laymen. (*Comp. II:* Concerning tithes [*De decimis*];[75] X: Concerning tithes, first-fruits, and oblations [*De decimis, primitiis, et oblationibus*])
4. Condemnation of the heretical sects spreading over regions in southern France: no one should grant refuge in his territory or offer assistance to members of these groups, nor should anyone have commercial dealing with them. If these heretics, who ought to be sought out, are seized, they should be kept in custody by catholic princes, and their goods ought to be confiscated. (*Comp. I:* Concerning heretics [*De hereticis*]; X: lacking)
5. Priests should not be obligated to pay an annual salary for their cure. (*Comp. I:* That prelates should not grant their functions or churches to others in return for an annual payment [*Ne prelati vices suas vel ecclesias aliis sub annuo pretio concedant*]; X: same, with the word "others" lacking, and *census* instead of *pretium* [*Ne prelati vices suas vel ecclesias sub annuo censu concedant*])
6. No payment should be demanded from those entering religious life, and chaplaincies should not be sold annually. A fee is not to be exacted from anyone to whom such an office is assigned, for this is simony; but neither should any charge be made for burial, or for anointing with chrism and oil. (*Comp. I:* Concerning simony, and that nothing should be demanded or promised for spiritual things [*De simonia et ne aliquid pro spiritualibus exigatur vel promittatur*]; X: same)
7. Deans or archpriests are not to perform the duties of bishops or archdeacons. (Same as for c. 5)
8. No one after professing religious vows is permitted to go to study medicine or secular law. If anyone does, and does not return to his cloister within two months, he is to be considered excommunicated, and is not to be heard in any case in which he acts as an advocate. If he returns to his cloister, he is to be the last in rank, and loses all hope of promotion, except by papal dispensation. (*Comp. I:* That clerics and monks should not occupy themselves with secular business [*Ne clerici vel monachi secularibus negotiis se immisceant*]; X: same)
9. Ordinations made by Victor IV, and other schismatics and heretics, are declared void. (Lacking)
"10." This is a lengthy decree emphasizing the immunity of ecclesiastical property. The canon condemns violators, as well as those who receive them as guests or have commercial dealing with them. (*Comp. II:* Concerning the immunity of churches and cemeteries [*De immunitate ecclesiae et cimiterii*]; X: lacking).

Since this text is not transmitted by Boso, but does appear in several decretal collections, a critical edition is of greater importance than in the previous instances.[76] This, plus its possible yet uncertain association with the 1163 council, makes a summary of each of its provisions impractical. It is sufficient to note that the decree relates to situations in both urban and rural areas, and seems directed toward controlling the seigneurs and their agents, especially military deputies.

This body of legislation does not focus in an obvious way on questions arising from schism, and as such can be contrasted with the decrees from Pope Urban II's synod at Piacenza in 1095.[77] The Council of Piacenza met at the height of the struggles with the imperially supported Pope Clement III, and concentrated on questions relating to schismatic clergy and their influence. These issues had vexed Urban from the beginning of his reign, and the conciliar solutions were landmarks, taken into many canonical collections including the *Decretum* of Gratian.[78] This attention in 1095 to such problems may explain the absence of further debate about them in later councils during similarly turbulent periods. No rulings of that sort appear in the conciliar corpus of Innocent II, for example, whose pontificate saw both schism and frequent papal councils.[79]

Yet Alexander did use Tours to reiterate other themes long familiar in the canonical tradition. Why he apparently chose to ignore issues engendered by the Church's divided state is unknown. Perhaps those matters held little practical interest for a council meeting in friendly territory and attended largely by sympathetic prelates, whereas at Piacenza the abnormal institutional and pastoral conditions which the schism had produced in northern Italy could not be ignored.[80] France in 1163 had not suffered in this way. But as Robert Benson has written, "every canonist of the generations after 1140 was schooled in the *Decretum*."[81] It would be of great interest to know if Gratian's work was used as a reference tool during the preparations for the council at Tours, and, if so, precisely how this influenced the choice of legislative themes for the synod.

Cardinal Boso wrote that the assembly at Tours reaffirmed "apostolic decisions" (*apostolica constituta corroborata sunt*) and then promulgated the nine new canons which he recited.[82] The *Continuatio Aquicinctina* for the *Chronicon* of Sigebert of Gembloux amplifies the first part of this by relating that in the 1163 council Alexander "renewed and confirmed the decrees of his predecessors" (*decreta predecessorum suorum renovavit et confirmavit*).[83] These reiterated but unspecified items might have included the conciliar statutes of the previous year from Montpellier, although at least one of Boso's "new" decrees, c. 8, existed in the 1162 proceedings.[84] Since the Montpellier canons are lost, their use at Tours cannot be evaluated, but in one instance a problem which does not reappear in 1163 is known to have been treated in the former assembly, as will be considered below.

Perhaps Boso's concept of novelty meant rulings enacted since Alexander became pope. The *Continuatio Aquicinctina* supports this assumption, and "new" canons, therefore, would include material repeated from Montpellier. The reaffirmed "apostolic decisions" then would be either a corpus of pre-Alexandrian canons, perhaps chosen for their relevance to the times, or a sweeping ratification, defined or undefined, of earlier papal legislation.

A renewal of this sort provides one explanation (other than simply its unwieldy length), for the *Vita Alexandri*'s omission of "c. 10," if the provision does belong at Tours. Despite its opening—"Since it is expedient to discover new remedies for new maladies . . ."[85]—Boso could have viewed the decree as a series of particular applications of a familiar theme: the special character of things ecclesiastical. The Peace of God would be an apt title under which to register this subject. A letter of Pope Innocent III to the archbishop of Auch, for example, later inserted into the *Compilatio quinta* under title 17 of book 1 (*De treuga et pace*), complained of those who "disturb the peace, not differentiating between sacred and profane they disrupt and ravage both ecclesiastical and worldly goods."[86] The so-called tenth canon begins similarly by defining proper action when clerics learn that the Church's holdings have been seized.

If the decree is authentic, this sort of explanation for its absence in the *Vita* is possible. But it must be noted quickly that similar reductions are applicable, without great ingenuity, to the texts which Boso does admit. As the subsequent paragraphs illustrate, these rulings can be deemed variations of fundamental ideas readily educible from the Church's legal dossier. Perhaps an explanation preferable to topical redundancy for Boso's neglect of this canon is the possibility that it was not transmitted directly from the council. Despite the inscription, it could be a letter written while Alexander was in the city, or more likely, given the attribution, it might be a conciliar text from a local gathering soon after the papal assembly and perhaps in the vicinity of Tours, which repromulgated the decisions of the earlier synod.

A situation analogous to this proposal can be extracted from the sources for the council in 1095 at Clermont.[87] The *Pax Dei* was affirmed at that gathering. Several lists of abbreviations of the decrees mention it, including a synopsis which may harbor official statements, the so-called *Polycarpus-Cencius* account. But a lengthy document of specific rules, bearing distinct connections with Tours, also survives, introduced as the "Peace confirmed . . . in the Council of Clermont." In all likelihood this text derives only indirectly from Clermont. It probably originated at a subsequent regional meeting near or at Tours, which renewed the papal decrees with a local flavor. Although geographical evidence is lacking, "c. 10" may have been drafted in a diocesan or provincial synod, based on a general reaffirmation from Pope Alexander's council of the special character of ecclesiastical property.

Nearly a century ago, Wilhelm von Giesebrecht wrote in this way of the 1163 legislation:

A number of canons from Tours are known. They address themselves to simoniacal damage in the Church, clerical usury, the selling of churches and ecclesiastical goods to laymen, the heretical sects spreading over southern France from Toulouse, monks who desert the cloister in order to study medicine and civil law, and so on. Most of these regulations are neither new nor of great significance.[88]

This simplistic characterization encompasses cc. 6, 2, 3, 4, and 8 (according to the enumeration of Boso). Von Giesebrecht is correct, if he meant to assert that many of the ideas in these rulings are not new. Severe condemnations of simony and of general lay interference with things ecclesiastical were prime tenets of the late eleventh-century reformers; "That it is not permitted for clerics or laymen to demand usury is proven by the authority of Gelasius [Pope Gelasius I, 492–96] and others"—thus wrote Gratian in his introduction to the fourth question of *Causa* 14; Innocent II had decreed that monks and regular canons should not pursue civil law or medicine for temporal gain;[89] and so on. But to declare summarily that because the provisions from Tours echo traditional concerns they are "neither new nor of great significance," is to miss their importance for the twelfth- and thirteenth-century Church.

Such an assessment disregards, in the first place, any novel responses which might be proposed for old difficulties. The second and fourth canons offer excellent examples. Pope Eugene III had already declared that usury occurs when anyone retains the revenues of a pledge which has been given as security for a loan, if the income gained exceeds the amount of the loan.[90] But this ruling had scant circulation in canonical collections, and it reached neither the *Quinque compilationes* nor the Gregorian *Decretales*. The second canon from Tours reiterates that position, but then qualifies it, permitting clerics to retain such interest if the pledge was an ecclesiastical benefice which in this way could be bought back from lay control. Writing at the end of the twelfth century, in his own commentary to his *Comp. I,* Bernard of Pavia said that it "seems astonishing that when a layman has an ecclesiastical benefice, clerics can gather the fruit of that benefice beyond the principal (of a loan)."[91] In other words, Alexander permitted the Church to receive what generally is considered usury. Bernard explained this new concept by remarking that "it is not done out of greed, but so that something in this manner can be redeemed from lay control,"[92] that is the cleric does not achieve a personal profit. The decree against heretics also is a landmark. The first of several papal statements against the Cathars, it has been said to have "laid down the basic principles on which the Inquisition was later to be founded."[93]

A comparison of the entire series of canons from Tours with the relevant portions of Gratian's *Decretum* might reveal additional innovations. But novel content aside, excepting the ad hoc condemnation of aberrant orders in c. 9, all of the decrees were absorbed into various decretal collections including the important *Quinque compilationes.* Apart from the discussion of heretics (which was quickly amplified by later papal statements), "c. 10," and again c. 9, the remaining seven texts entered the *Decretales* of Gregory IX,[94] becoming familiar statements in a solidified canonical tradition. The legislation promulgated at Tours is important not only for what was said in 1163, but also for the way in which the Church preserved what was said.

EXCURSUS: THE CANONS OF MONTPELLIER, 1162

The uncertain relationship of these decrees to the gathering at Tours has been noted.[95] A detailed treatment of the issue must be predicated upon discovering further information. No canons from Montpellier are known; and they probably did not penetrate into the decretal literature since no traces remain in the extant compilations. The reason for this neglect could be that the provisions were reformulated at more substantial gatherings, such as Tours or Lateran III, or in decretal letters.

A legatine council at Montpellier in 1195 offers the only known evidence of their existence.[96] In two cases, the local papal gathering thirty-three years earlier was recalled as a precedent, both times in conjunction either with Tours or Lateran III.[97] These references probably are indicative more of civic or territorial pride than of legal content. Clerics studying civil law and medicine were dealt with "according to the decree on the matter promulgated by Pope Alexander in council at Montpellier and Tours." The synod also condemned "all heretics," and assorted thieves and pirates including those selling military supplies to the Saracens, "on the model of the decrees against such action from the Lateran council." Their goods should be confiscated; they should endure servitude; and secular princes who have been informed by the Church but who have not bothered to move against them *(jurisdictionem temporalem in eos non curaverunt exercere),* should be censured as one of them, "just as it was stated in the aforementioned Lateran council, and in the synod which the aforesaid Pope Alexander is known to have celebrated at Montpellier."

The sources alleged from Lateran III are unclear. Probably some combination of cc. 24, 26, and 27 was intended.[98] If Tours' neglect in the second of the two passages cited does denote anything other than the frame of reference of the Montpellier fathers, it probably means that the 1163 synod did not legislate about *maritimae urbes*[99] and the Saracens, an assumption which the extant sources for the council at Tours corroborate. Such issues obviously were more urgent on the Mediterranean coast than in the Loire Valley. Alexander must have considered those questions in 1162—Boso reported that while at Montpellier the pope met with a Saracen prince[100]—and not again in council until 1179 at the Lateran.

*The following, kindly brought to the author's attention by Dr. Martin Bertram, can be added to the list of MSS of canons of Tours (pp. 44–46):*
*Paris, Bibliothèque nat. MS lat. 2995, fols. 22v–24r, thirteenth century, cc. 5–8, 3, 1, 2, 4: see* Catalogue général des manuscrits latins, *3 (Paris 1952) 380–81.*
*Wolfenbüttel, 404.4 (11) Novi, one page, thirteenth/fourteenth century fragment of what must have been a decretal collection, with authentic and inauthentic Tours texts, including "c. 10": see Hans Butzmann,* Die mittelalterlichen Handschriften der Gruppen Extravagantes, Novi, und Novissimi, Kataloge der Herzog August Bibliothek Wolfenbüttel, *15 (Frankfurt am Main 1972) 224.*

# 6

## The Conciliar Acts

The pressures which engendered conciliar canons often are hidden from modern investigators. Unless the texts themselves give hints, as in the fourth canon of the synod at Tours, which treats the Cathars,[1] the circumstantial background for the decrees reduces to the truism that "X condemned implies X." But a synod was not limited to promulgating general laws. When, for example, Pope Innocent II reportedly claimed in the Lateran Council of 1139 that "it belongs to the Roman pontiff to pacify dissent, and wisely to arrange and order what is confused,"[2] he was designating a great range of synodal operations. Ecclesiastical business such as excommunications, theological inquiry, and hearing and judging specific cases demanded attention in councils, and in these instances the historical context often can be perceived.

The relationship usually is obscure between the canons and this mélange of processes which are termed the "acts."[3] Perhaps the canons were presented to an assembly by the pope, while most other business, with the exception, conceivably, of excommunications, was initiated by the participants. Yet in place of tranquil acceptance, the proposed legislation might trigger lively debates;[4] and statutes certainly could be prompted by inquiries from the floor.[5] If several cases involving the same abuse were brought before the pontiff in a council, it might inspire a general decree on the matter. At other times, an issue intended for canonical formulation could remain unformulated, either locked in a committee or because of inconclusive plenary debate, and thus belong to the *acta* and not become part of the legislation. Something of this sort may have occurred at Tours with the Christological episode to be considered below.

A striking feature of twelfth-century ecclesiastical government was Rome's ability to foster confidence in papal justice throughout Europe, and hence

56

to expand its jurisdiction. As noted in the first chapter, synods became less and less essential to this development throughout the century;[6] yet whenever they did convene, these gatherings provided an opportune moment to treat a substantial number of petitions. Many of the participants would be eager to ventilate in such a forum local ecclesiastical problems about jurisdiction, finances, and so forth.[7] How agenda were put together at twelfth-century councils is uncertain; but a pontiff would be likely to handle as many questions as time, energy, and political considerations allowed, given the fees to be gained[8] and the desire to appear a great if not universal administrator. These two factors were especially important during a schism, when money could be short,[9] and when popularity as a court of appeal would help measure the competitors' respective strength. The paucity of sources for Victor IV, and the complications of imperial pressures, obscure this aspect of his reign.[10] For Alexander, however, the royal prohibition against English clergy bringing disputes to Tours is perhaps an indirect witness to the vigor of his administrative intentions.

A few of the issues treated in the council at Tours have echoes in Alexander's correspondence dispatched thereafter. This includes the uproars about seating analyzed in Chapter 4, disputes the pontiff surely would have preferred not to hear. These squabbles were seemingly unpremeditated, and were capable of erupting with the slightest provocation from deep metropolitan, abbatial, and national tensions. But they do indicate that despite the benefits of attracting cases during a schism, the endeavor was beset by an obvious peril. Any party whose arguments were rejected, and against whom a judgment was rendered, became a potential enemy. Even without turning traitor, a dissatisfied and voluble litigant could prove embarrassing to a council determined to be a show of strength and unity.[11] Furthermore, Alexander suffered with the specific problem that any question touching England could damage his relations with Henry II. Discretion of the sort visible in the seating disputes was needed constantly. Detailed records of the *acta* from Tours, had they survived, certainly would testify to the pope's diplomatic skill.

A glance through the pertinent pages of JL, or the various Göttingen *Pontificia-Papsturkunden* volumes,[12] provides an idea of the number and type of decisions rendered by Alexander in late May and early June. The problem of relating all of these judgments to activity in the council has been mentioned in the discussion of abbatial attendance.[13] Not every letter from the time of the gathering, or shortly thereafter, embodies a synodal decision.[14] Conversely, absence of such a reference probably is not sufficient evidence to dismiss consideration on the floor of the assembly, or in a subcommittee. The significant factor in recording a judgment would be papal involvement. The locus of that involvement might be neglected, although to

a modern mind it seems surprising that a party would not insist on words
such as *in concilio,* if they could.

The process of sifting what happened in the council from contemporary
events in the city is illustrated by some incidents concerning Thomas Becket.
The fascination that this man exerted, on both his own and subsequent ages,
makes these examples more than routinely interesting. His reported secret
resignation of the see of Canterbury obviously did not occur in the synod.[15]
According to Herbert of Bosham, however, Thomas successfully petitioned
Alexander at Tours to renew "several privileges" for Canterbury.[16] When
did this happen? Herbert mentioned it prior to reporting the pope's farewell
to the Canterbury delegation, after noting that "the council had been celebrated for several days." The affair could have been part of the synod, but
Herbert does not say that it was.

Equally vague is the chronology of another request from Thomas to the
pope, this time concerning Gilbert Foliot. A letter from Alexander to the
archbishop, datable only between 1164 and 1170, recalled that Thomas at
Tours had desired to obtain from Bishop Gilbert of London a profession of
obedience.[17] The pontiff did not specify whether this wish was expressed
publicly or privately, remarking only that "while you were with us for the
celebration of the council at Tours, we remember that you wished to obtain.
. . ."[18] The non-public alternative is much more likely, given the restric-
tions imposed by Henry II on his clerics. But Thomas might have believed
that his request did not involve carrying a dispute before the pope—the
activity which Henry had forbidden—but only pursuing an established Canterbury custom of securing proper allegiance.[19]

However the matter arose, Alexander's reaction was negative. Gilbert,
recently transferred from Hereford to London, already had professed obedience from his former see to Thomas's predecessor Archbishop Theobald.
The pope deemed this to be sufficient, explaining to Thomas in the undated
letter that it was not the Roman Church's practice to require a second profession from a transferred bishop.[20] But did the issue reach the floor of the
synod? The evidence does not permit an answer.

Hugh of Poitiers wrote that "many . . . controversies were brought forth
from all sides and resolved in the council."[21] A great number of these cannot be recognized from their form of survival, or have no extant record;
but the following *acta* can be placed in the gathering on the basis of primary sources. Only the final two merit commentary here.

1. Excommunication of the schismatics: to be discussed in the following
chapter.

2. Consecration by Pope Alexander of John, treasurer at York, as bishop
of Poitiers.[22]

3. Papal intervention of an undefined sort in an episcopal schism at Pamplona: Chapter 3 above, note 83.

4. Bishop Maurice of Paris advanced a claim against the abbey of St.-Germain-des-Prés, asserting that he had a certain right (jurisdiction? the words are *quoddam ius*) over that house. Since St.-Germain long had possessed a papal exemption, Maurice was asked to indicate any previous Roman pontiffs who had recognized his rights, that is he was being asked to produce substantiating documents.[23] Since he could not—and Alexander confides to the monks in what could be irony that "we do not think that he can"—the claims were dismissed.[24]

5. A controversy was ventilated between Cluny and Bishop John of Maguelonne, concerning the rights and obligations of the Cluniac priory of St.-Pierre near Montpellier. Although both sides produced papal letters, the matter remained unresolved. By Alexander's command, and with the consent of the parties, the dispute was handed over to a committee: Cardinals Humbald of Ostia, Bernard of Porto, William of S. Pietro in Vincoli, and Manfred of S. Giorgio in Velabro. The resulting *concordia,* dated 13 June 1163, established in detail the proper relations between bishop and monks.[25]

6. An attempt by Thomas Becket to have Anselm of Canterbury canonized. This initiative had been carefully prepared. A *Vita Anselmi,* seemingly composed by John of Salisbury, and a catalogue of miracles were offered to the council for inspection.[26] Anselm had been patiently loyal to the Gregorian program of ecclesiastical reform, enduring abuse and exile for his refusal to bend to the royal will. His memory was personally dear to Thomas,[27] and the attempted canonization could have been motivated by a desire to balance the similar honor recently accorded to King Edward the Confessor.[28]

But even with a supporting dossier, the request was not granted. "Deferred" or "side-stepped" is a better term than "refused."[29] Alexander may have been sympathetic to the idea, but it was explosive. King Henry probably would not have welcomed Anselm's sainthood under any circumstances, but how much less so if achieved through the initiative of the archbishop of Canterbury! Thomas and Alexander both must have realized that. The pope may have cautioned the archbishop accordingly, and the episode probably is an early sign of Thomas's strained and deteriorating relations with his monarch.[30]

As with the seating controversy, and the reaffirmation of Gilbert Foliot's obedience, in this case too Alexander had a reasoned explanation for his actions, or rather for his refusal to act. Church architecture and canonical tradition respectively were cited in the former instances.[31] The proposal for Anselm was set aside, the pontiff told Thomas in a letter soon thereafter,

because numerous other appeals for canonization had been advanced at the
same time.[32] Two other letters elaborate this.[33] Both were written in 1174,
and announce the canonization of St. Bernard of Clairvaux. Alexander related that while visiting Paris, which he did just before the council at Tours,
some important men (*magni quidam ac venerabiles viri*) had suggested that
Bernard be so honored at the forthcoming gathering. The pope was favorably
inclined, but was unable to act because of a multitude of similar petitions
from others. Not everyone could have been satisfied *congruenter,* indicating
that some would have been dissatisfied. Alexander does not say so explicitly, but it is likely that a decision had been made to avoid offending any-
body on this issue. Under such a policy, even worthy candidates such as Bernard, and perhaps Anselm, were denied consideration.[34]

Whatever the pontiff thought of Anselm's qualifications, he washed his
hands of the matter by remitting it to Thomas for metropolitan action. The
archbishop should convene a provincial council—the suffragan bishops,
abbots, and other religious persons of the province are specified—and therein consider the case. The pope is prepared to follow the resulting decision.
Anselm's hagiological fate thus became an English issue, and even more
pointedly, an affair of the province of Canterbury. Any ensuing conflict
would involve King Henry, Thomas, and perhaps Roger of York, but not
the king and Pope Alexander.

It is unknown whether Thomas acted on the question.[35] The imminent
controversy with his monarch may have precluded it, although R. W. Southern, on the basis of a twelfth-century calendar (ante 1171) from Christ
Church, Canterbury, is inclined to the opinion that "the formalities of
canonization were completed" before the archbishop went into exile.[36]
Whether or not this is so, it was Thomas himself who ultimately impeded
the popularity that he had striven to foster for Anselm. His death, and its
reception, overshadowed all possible veneration for any of his predecessors.
Notwithstanding honors which might have been gained for Anselm in 1163-
64, from the 1170s to the Reformation the great saint at Canterbury was
not Anselm but Thomas.

7. In his *Eulogium ad Papam Alexandrum tertium,* John of Cornwall
provided a glimpse into an aspect of the council which must have been of
especial importance, but whose record has virtually disappeared.[37] The for-
tuitous survival of this text permits the fragmentary quality of the conciliar
sources to be reiterated. The issue was an ancient one, the relation of divinity
and humanity in Christ. If the *Eulogium* is trustworthy (its modern editor
has termed it "the most informative treatise on the extremely fundamental
christological controversy in the Twelfth Century"),[38] the conciliar discussion was heated. The fifth-century Chalcedonian Christology, which decided

that Christ possesses two natures in one person, "which exist in this one Person without confusion, without change, without division, and without separation,"[39] had been debated bitterly before, especially in the East. As Harnack has said, "The Church knew what it wanted to do—to unite contradictions. . . ."[40]

The twelfth-century dispute in the Latin Church focused on what has been termed a "nihilistic" interpretation of this hypostatic union.[41] The "nihilists" were blamed for annihilating the humanity of Christ. As John of Cornwall put it, the discussions at Tours centered on the dogma of those who asserted that "Christ is not someone as man" (*Christus non est aliquis homo*), and that "Christ as man is not anything" (*Christus secundum quod homo non est aliquid*).[42] According to D. E. Luscombe, the problem "was not the concrete humanity of Christ or his psychological personality as man, but the dialectical qualification of that humanity which was not itself a person and which therefore seemed to some not to be qualifiable as anything."[43]

The origins of these views, their relation to Peter Lombard, and their ultimate rejection by the Church, pertain to the general history of medieval theology. Of interest here is the burden which this issue placed on Alexander III at a time of crisis. Master Roland, the future Pope Alexander, had been a student of Peter Abelard as well as of Gratian.[44] He was, as Beryl Smalley wrote, "an intellectual in politics."[45] As a master of theology, Roland had composed a collection of *Sententie,* among which he wrote that "we say that Christ is a third Person of the Trinity, but as God, not as man, especially since as man He is not a person . . . nor anything. . . ."[46] This "fruit de l'enseignement abélardien," as Joseph de Ghellinck has characterized that point of view,[47] obviously heightened the tensions in the debate at Tours.

Unfortunately, the episode is most obscure. John of Cornwall may not even be reporting from personal experience,[48] and all he says is that the exchanges were spirited and inconclusive. N. M. Häring observes that "although no final decision was reached at the synod, it could at least be claimed as a victory of a sort by all parties."[49] Walter of St.-Victor could assert, therefore, that in the council Alexander "condemned the heresy . . . in which Christ is said to be nothing as man."[50] John of Cornwall's account makes that unlikely, and Walter probably is a victim of either faulty information or wishful thinking. The first evidence of a definite pronouncement on Alexander's part comes in 1170, when the pontiff finally condemned "the depraved doctrine that Christ as a man is not anything."[51] As de Ghellinck has noted, "It was a total break with the Christological nihilism of Abelard, by which he [Alexander] had been influenced during his teaching at Bologna, thirty years earlier."[52]

The *Vita Alexandri* ignores these theological problems. Commencing the work, Boso does remark that the pontiff was "supremely eloquent, well-versed in both divine and human writings, and distinguished for their most penetrating interpretation."[53] Considering his volte-face on the question, the details of the Christological struggle could have been embarrassing in a book aiming to portray "Alexander as the single-minded hero who had no thought other than to restore and preserve the unity of the Church Universal."[54] But this quest for unity could have helped to elicit the inconclusive theological discussion at Tours. It may have been politic to avoid specificity on that volatile question, just as with the equally touchy matters of seating and sainthood.

But given Roland's previous stance on the issue, and the issue itself, there were special complications. Politics notwithstanding, it may have been intellectually appropriate, and invigorating, to allow all sides a full hearing. The religious problems at stake should not be deemed inconsequential for a scholar who previously had struggled with "the task of accommodating what was useful in Abelard's teachings within the framework of an acceptable structure of theological thought."[55] Hefele-Leclercq succinctly observed that the debate at Tours was inconclusive, "because the question did not seem to him (the pontiff) to have been resolved."[56] That is appealing; but as de Ghellinck wrote of the post-1163 stages in this drama, the sources are more conducive to speculation than to "une idée bien complète des événements."[57]

# 7

## The Council of Tours
## and the Schism

The initial chapter sketched the events leading to the council at Tours; chapters 2–4 and 6 treated the known synodal activities; and the fifth chapter analyzed the decrees, both their preservation and their content. An assessment can now be made, in conclusion, of the council's impact on the Alexandrian-Victorine schism, and on the concomitant political situation.

Just as "church" and "state" were intertwined throughout medieval society generally, so in considering the assembly in 1163 it is difficult if not impossible to separate them. All contention denotes vying for objectives; but the medieval *regnum-sacerdotium* battles, including that waged between Frederick and Alexander, often were competitions for predominant authority over spheres of activity which, because of society's structure, were not the exclusive domain of either "church" or "state." The 1163 council was both a political parliament and a religious conference, and it formed a microcosm of a society whose bishops frequently were both secular lords and pastors.

The discussions in the previous chapters about seating, canonization, and the theological debate reveal specific incidents of this confluence. The historian would like further details about these episodes, and especially about what people thought of them. Did the participants view the synod more as a political or a religious gathering? That question might have made little sense in the 1160s, but were it possible to conduct a survey, no more interesting respondent could be found than Thomas Becket. He had been both a statesman and a churchman of high position, although not simultaneously, and he surely would recognize political actions even if wrapped in religious garb. The extant shreds of evidence reveal Thomas very active at Tours on behalf of Canterbury. But how did the council strike him? Was it true, as Wolter following Foreville has asserted, that the event "deepened in Thomas the awareness that the interests of the Roman Church and the Church of Canterbury were identical"?[1] No response is possible without knowing things such as which Canterbury privileges were renewed at Tours,[2] how Thomas reacted to the canonical legislation and to the offensive against the schismatics,[3] and whether he did or did not secretly resign his see into Alexander's hands and thence receive it again. There are, unfortunately, no answers.

Geoffrey Barraclough has written that during the period of Alexander's struggles with Frederick Barbarossa, "the strain imposed on the loyalty [to Frederick] of many leading prelates was . . . great."[4] The impressive display at Tours, with its renewed condemnations of the Victorine leaders, must have caused more than a few second thoughts in the Empire about the direction of events, although here again specific evidence is lacking. The *Continuatio Aquicinctina* for the *Chronicon* of Sigebert of Gembloux named some of those opposition leaders whom the assembly stigmatized:[5] Rainald of Dassel,[6] chancellor and archbishop of Cologne; Abbot Hugh,[7] the Victorine representative in an abbatial schism at Cluny; and Conrad of Wittelsbach,[8] archbishop-elect of Mainz. This list must be incomplete,[9] and the most conspicuous omission is the emperor, a fact that has not been neglected by historians.[10]

It does appear to have escaped notice, however, that Stephen of Rouen testified to Frederick's lenient treatment at the council. In the *Draco Normannicus,* Alexander III is made to recite the following apropos of the condemnations: "We exclude the emperor, whom I wish to reconcile to us on these matters."[11] The pope is depicted, therefore, as hoping that Frederick will consent to the proceedings against the others. Victor and his allies have been sentenced, but if the emperor forsakes that company, he will be shown mercy. Further information about the diplomatic initiatives emerging from the assembly at Tours has been obliterated, but there is little question that an effort was in progress to draw Frederick away from Victor.[12] If that succeeded, the entire Victorine party quickly would be dragged after him into Alexander's obedience. Whether the Alexandrians had reason to think that the emperor could be interested is unknown. But the hopes were real, and Arnulf of Lisieux expressed them in this way:[13]

My lords and fathers, we have certain faithful helpers: the grace of the celestial community, your merits and prayers, and the faith and devotion of catholic kings, who verbally assent with us to catholic unity and pursue it by deed—almost all (rulers) who are considered Christian (thus behave).[14] In comparison to such a multitude, one exception is insignificant, yet there is a solitary exception. . . . But he, too, through God's mercy, will be converted and live, since he is laudable among earthly princes for prudence and virtue, unless he has decided to place his own glory above divine glory. If only he would humble himself under God's powerful hand, and realize that the Church's lordship is preeminent to his own. If only he would understand that if he confesses that Christ, the bridegroom of the Church, is *dominus,* he also must confess that the Church, which is the bride, is nothing less than *domina.*

Frederick might be mildly flattered by some of this, but would disdain the final sentences; and his insistence on arbitration to end the schism, and his support for Paschal III in 1164 upon Victor's death, indicate a rejection of any overtures which Alexander made after Tours.[15] But did the emperor have any choice?[16] If Alexander were recognized as pope and emerged from the schism victorious, the imperialists could hardly hope to reach acceptable solutions to other disputed questions. The ecclesiastical breach was only a manifestation of the deep and persistent incompatibility between medieval *regnum* and *sacerdotium.* In 1163 the Alexandrians were prepared to admit Frederick into their communion; but for intelligible reasons they were unable to recognize the importance to Frederick of his claims to authority over those "imperial" things which touched "Roman ecclesiastical" things. Alexander and his followers cannot be accused of radical solutions to chronic problems. As Arnulf reminded the fathers assembled at Tours:[17]

He (Frederick) has a special reason why he ought to recognize the lordship (*domina*) of the Church, otherwise he will appear most clearly guilty of ingratitude. For if we turn to past history, it will be certain that his predecessors received the empire not through any other authority (*ius*) than the singular grace of the holy Roman Church. Princes, therefore, cannot claim greater authority than what the dignity of the bestower has conferred on them.

If Frederick had betrayed Victor, the gathering at Tours would be remembered as a great diplomatic success. Since that did not occur, the council easily can be forgotten among the subsequent political maneuvers and military campaigns which took place between 1163 and 1179. The assembly did not launch a crusade, nor did it mark the end of a great controversy as did the Lateran synods of 1123, 1139, and 1179. In fact, the shortage of information about the operations and juridical proceedings at Tours may be a result of this inconclusiveness. Ordinary matters can become obscured in extraordinary and especially in oppressive circumstances; and it must not be forgotten that Pope Alexander had to contend with the Becket crisis soon thereafter, and while still battling with Frederick.

Yet despite the ease with which it is possible to speculate about why this assembly and its place in history must be dominated by the political atmosphere of the 1160s, that is not the entire story. In contrast to the Council

of Montpellier, the synod at Tours was represented in the late twelfth-
century canonical books by a series of important decrees. Notwithstanding
the perils of arguments from silence, this program apparently owed little to
the turmoil of the period.[18] Nor did that confusion prevent its survival, although the mechanism of this preservation, in all likelihood, will never be
fully transparent.

Boso's account of the 1163 council suggests that he too saw the meeting
as important apart from and beyond the papal-imperial strife. Despite Peter
Munz's observation that "in Boso's view Alexander had no other aim than
to restore and preserve the unity of the Church; and Frederick had no other
aim than to destroy that unity,"[19] the *Vita Alexandri* tells nothing of the
assembly at Tours, other than the attendance figures and the decrees,
neglecting even its actions against the Victorines. This format may be func-
tional, indicating Boso's use of official records,[20] perhaps well after 1163
when the synod's political machinations were obsolete or even forgotten. But
might it not have been Boso's desire to exalt Alexander and his office by a
conspicuous neglect of the raging battles? No reader of the *Vita* can decide
that the council did not treat such questions, given what comes before and
after, but perhaps the cardinal hoped that his presentation would stress
something else. By depicting a great juridical assembly with Alexander at its
head, Boso may have intended to reveal papal solicitude for the day-to-day
welfare of the Church, despite a world deep in crisis. Such a pope is the
universal pastor and pontiff "whose authority," as Norman Zacour has written, "needed no conciliar confirmation," but who appeared in the council
"in more solemn and public fashion [to] exercise that moral and spiritual
leadership which was his supreme duty."[21] How is it possible, Boso might
ask, to prefer the sycophantic Victor IV to a religious leader of this sort?
That the *Vita*'s unembellished portrait of the council was meant to convey
this image is suppositional, although the idea probably would please Boso
if, indeed, it had not occurred to him. Alexander hardly could object to it
either, even if in writing to the bishops in the province of Salzburg soon
afterward he did note his accomplishments at Tours in terms both of "many
decisions for the peace and growth of all Christendom" and the excommunication of the schismatics.[22]

But the council did not end nor shorten the schism, and the Church's turmoil continued, compounded by new dangers such as the Becket dispute,
for fifteen more years. It could be wondered, finally, whether the gathering
at Tours did not prolong the crisis. Whatever initiatives emerged from it
aiming to placate Frederick were unsuccessful. The reasons for this failure
probably are rooted in the haughty and essentially uncompromising nature
of those efforts.[23] Few things serve better to fan smouldering emotions into

anger than overtures of toleration, however sincere, which nonetheless are patronizing or even disdainful. Both the Roman pontiff and the Roman emperor were representatives of prideful traditions, and in 1163 Alexander and Frederick were far from battle weary. For these reasons, the Council of Tours's legacy was not a political settlement, but instead the canons recorded by Boso and perpetuated by the decretalists throughout Latin Christendom.

# Bibliography

The bibliography which follows is to enable readers to understand the footnotes. It contains all titles cited in abbreviated form, but it is not a complete list of relevant sources and literature. Medieval works are cited under the name of the editor when the commentary or introduction has been used more frequently than the medieval text itself. Cross-references are supplied where appropriate.

Annales du Mont-Saint-Michel: *see* Delisle.

Arnulf of Lisieux: *see* Barlow, and Giles.

Avril, Joseph. "La province de Tours après le IV$^e$ concile du Latran, Les *'Articuli missi archiepiscopo Turonensi . . .'* (Nantes, Bibl. mun., ms. 36, fo 90-91)." *Annuarium historiae conciliorum* 6 (1974) 291-306.

Baldwin, Marshall W. *Alexander III and the Twelfth Century.* The Popes through History, 3. Glen Rock, N. J. 1968.

Baluze, Étienne. *Miscellanea novo ordine digesta.* Edited by G. D. Mansi. 4 vols. Lucca 1761-64.

Barlow, Frank, ed. *The Letters of Arnulf of Lisieux.* Camden Society, 3rd ser., 61. London 1939.

Baronius, Caesar. *Annales ecclesiastici.* 38 vols. Lucca 1738-59.

Barrow, Geoffrey W. S. *The Acts of Malcolm IV, King of Scots 1153-1165.* Regesta regum Scottorum, 1. Edinburgh 1960.

——. *The Acts of William I, King of Scots 1165-1214.* Regesta regum Scottorum, 2. Edinburgh 1971.

Benson, Robert L. *The Bishop-Elect.* Princeton 1968.

Binius, Severinus. *Concilia generalia et provincialia.* 4 vols. Cologne 1618.

Boso: see *Vita Alexandri,* and Munz.

Brooke, C. N. L. "Canons of English Church Councils in Early Decretal Collections." *Traditio* 13 (1957) 471-80.

Brooke, Z. N., Adrian Morey, and C. N. L. Brooke. *The Letters and Charters of Gilbert Foliot.* Cambridge 1967.

Carré de Busserolle, J.-X. *Dictionnaire géographique, historique, et biographique d'Indre-et-Loire et de l'ancienne province de Touraine.* 6 vols. Tours 1878-84.

Cheney, C. R. "Textual Problems of the English Provincial Canons." In *La Critica del Testo: Atti del 2° Congresso internazionale della Società Italiana di Storia del Diritto,* vol. 1 (Florence 1971), 165-88.

―――, and Mary G. Cheney. *The Letters of Pope Innocent III (1198-1216) concerning England and Wales.* Oxford 1967.

Cheney, Mary G. "The Recognition of Pope Alexander III: Some Neglected Evidence." *English Historical Review* 84 (1969) 474-97.

Chodorow, Stanley. *Christian Political Theory and Church Politics in the Mid-Twelfth Century.* Berkeley and Los Angeles 1972.

Classen, Peter. *Gerhoch von Reichersberg.* Wiesbaden 1960.

COD=*Conciliorum oecumenicorum decreta.* Edited by Giuseppe Alberigo et al. 2nd ed. Freiburg 1962.

*Comp. I, II, III, IV, V: see* Friedberg, *Quinque compilationes antiquae.*

Constable, Giles. *The Letters of Peter the Venerable,* vol. 2. Harvard Historical Studies, 78. Cambridge, Mass. 1967.

Cottineau, L. H. *Répertoire topo-bibliographique des abbayes et prieurés.* 3 vols. (vol. 3 prepared by G. Poras). Mâcon 1939-70.

Crabbe, Peter. *Concilia omnia,* vol. 2. Cologne 1551.

DBI=*Dizionario biografico degli Italiani.* In progress. Rome 1960- .

*Decretales: see* Gregory IX.

De Ghellinck, Joseph. *Le mouvement théologique du XIIe siècle.* 2nd ed. Museum Lessianum, Section historique, 10. Bruges 1948.

Delisle, Léopold. *Chronique de Robert de Torigni, abbé du Mont-Saint-Michel.* Société de l'histoire de Normandie, 3-4. 2 vols. Rouen 1872-73.

DHGE=*Dictionnaire d'histoire et de géographie ecclésiastiques.* In progress. Paris 1912- .

Dickinson, William C. *Scotland from the Earliest Times to 1603.* A New History of Scotland, 1. London 1965.

DTC=*Dictionnaire de théologie catholique.* 16 vols. Paris 1903-72.

Duchesne, Louis. *Le liber pontificalis.* Bibliothèque des Écoles françaises d'Athènes et de Rome, 2e sér., 3. 2 vols. Paris 1886-92.

Duggan, Charles. "From the Conquest to the Death of John." In *The English Church and the Papacy in the Middle Ages,* ed. Clifford H. Lawrence (New York 1965), 63-115.

―――. *Twelfth-Century Decretal Collections and Their Importance in English History.* University of London Historical Studies, 12. London 1963.

Engel, Johannes. *Das Schisma Barbarossas im Bistum und Hochstift Freising (1159-77).* Munich 1930.

Eyton, Robert W. *Court, Household and Itinerary of King Henry II.* London 1878.

Fabre, Paul, and Louis Duchesne. *Le Liber censuum.* Bibliothèque des Écoles françaises d'Athènes et de Rome, 2e sér., 6. 3 vols. (vol. 3 prepared by P. Fabre and G. Mollat). Paris 1889-1952.

Falkenstein, Ludwig. "Ein vergessener Brief Alexanders III. an einen 'Rex Hibernorum'." *Archivum historiae pontificiae* 10 (1972) 107-60.

*Fasti*=John Le Neve, *Fasti Ecclesiae Anglicanae, 1066–1300,* 2: *Monastic Cathedrals (Northern and Southern Provinces).* Compiled by Diana E. Greenway. London 1971.

*Fasti Scot.* =*Fasti Ecclesiae Scoticanae Medii Aevi ad annum 1638.* Compiled by D. E. R. Watt. 2nd draft. Scottish Record Society, n.s., 1. Edinburgh 1969.

Foreville, Raymonde. *L'Église et la royauté en Angleterre sous Henri II Plantagenet (1154–1189).* Paris 1943.

———. *Latran I, II, III et Latran IV.* Histoire des conciles oecuméniques, 6. Paris 1965.

Friedberg, Aemilius. CS=*Die Canones-Sammlungen zwischen Gratian und Bernhard von Pavia.* Leipzig 1897.

———. *Quinque compilationes antiquae.* Leipzig 1882.

Fuhrmann, Horst. "Das Ökumenische Konzil und seine historischen Grundlage." *Geschichte in Wissenschaft und Unterricht* 12 (1961) 672-95.


Gams, P. B. *Series episcoporum ecclesiae catholicae.* Regensburg 1873-86.

Geisthardt, Fritz. *Der Kämmerer Boso.* Historische Studien, 293. Berlin 1936.

Giles, J. A. *Arnulfi Lexoviensis episcopi epistolae.* Oxford 1844.

Girgensohn, Dieter. "Das Pisaner Konzil von 1135 in der Überlieferung des Pisaner Konzils von 1409." In *Festschrift für Hermann Heimpel,* vol. 2 (Göttingen 1972), 1063-1100.

Graesse, J. G. T., et al. *Orbis Latinus.* 2nd ed. by Friedrich Benedict (1909), revised by Helmut and Sophie-Charlotte Plechl. 3 vols. Braunschweig 1972.

Gratian. *Concordia discordantium canonum (=Decretum).* Edited by Aemilius Friedberg. *Corpus iuris canonici,* vol. 1. Leipzig 1879.

GP=*Germania pontificia.* Edited by Albert Brackmann. 3 vols. Berlin 1910-35.

Gregory IX. *Liber extravagantium decretalium (=Decretales).* Edited by Aemilius Friedberg. *Corpus iuris canonici,* vol. 2 (Leipzig 1881), 1-928.


Häring, Nicholas M. "John"="The *Eulogium ad Alexandrum Papam tertium* of John of Cornwall." *Mediaeval Studies* 13 (1951) 253-300.

———. "Notes"="Notes on the Council and the Consistory of Rheims (1148)." *Mediaeval Studies* 28 (1966) 39-59.

Hardouin, Jean. *Acta conciliorum.* 11 vols. Paris 1714-15.

Hauck, Albert. *Kirchengeschichte Deutschlands,* vol. 4. 6th ed. Berlin and Leipzig 1953.

HCH=*Handbook of Church History.* Edited by Hubert Jedin and John Dolan. Vol. 3: Friedrich Kempf et al., *The Church in the Age of Feudalism;* vol. 4: Hans-Georg Beck et al., *From the High Middle Ages to the Eve of the Reformation.* Trans. Anselm Biggs. New York and London 1969-70 (=*Handbuch der Kirchengeschichte,* ed. Hubert Jedin, vol. 3:1-2).

HE=*Histoire de l'église depuis les origines jusqu'à nos jours, publiée sous la direction de Augustin Fliche et Victor Martin.* Vol. 8: Augustin Fliche, *La Réforme grégorienne et la reconquête chrétienne (1057–1123).* Paris 1940. Vol. 9:1-2:

Augustin Fliche (part 1), Raymonde Foreville, and Jean Rousset de Pina, *Du premier Concile du Latran à l'avènement d'Innocent III (1123–1198)*. Paris 1944–53.

Hefele, Carl J., Joseph Hergenroether, and Henri Leclercq. *Histoire des conciles*. 8 vols. Paris 1907–21.

Heinemeyer, Walter. "Die Verhandlungen an der Saône im Jahre 1162." *Deutsches Archiv* 20 (1964) 155–89.

Heyer, Friedrich. Review article of Heinrich Singer, *Beiträge* (see below under Singer). ZRG, Kan. Abt. 3 (1913) 615–42.

———. Review article of Heinrich Singer, *Die Dekretalensammlung des Bernardus Compostellanus antiquus*. ZRG, Kan. Abt. 4 (1914) 583–608.

HL=Hefele et al.

Holtzmann, Walther. "KE"="Kanonistisches Ergänzungen zur *Italia pontificia*." *Quellen und Forschungen aus Italienischen Archiven und Bibliotheken* 37 (1957) 55–102; 38 (1958) 67–175.

———. "Register"="Die Register Papst Alexanders III. in den Händen der Kanonisten." *Quellen und Forschungen aus Italienischen Archiven und Bibliotheken* 30 (1940) 13–87.

———. "Simon"="Zu den Dekretalen bei Simon von Bisignano." *Traditio* 18 (1962) 450–59.

———. "Tanner"="Die Dekretalensammlungen des 12. Jahrhunderts, 1: Die Sammlung Tanner." In *Festschrift zur Feier des zweihundertjährigen Bestehens der Akademie der Wissenschaften Göttingen,* vol. 2 (Göttingen 1951), 83–145.

———, and Eric W. Kemp. *Papal Decretals Relating to the Diocese of Lincoln in the Twelfth Century.* Lincoln Record Society, 47. Hereford 1954.

IP=*Italia pontificia*. Edited by Paul Kehr. 9 vols. (vol. 9 prepared by Walther Holtzmann). Berlin 1906–62.

Janssen, Wilhelm. *Die päpstlichen Legaten in Frankreich vom Schisma Anaklets II. bis zum Tode Coelestins III. (1130–1198)*. Kölner historische Abhandlungen, 6. Cologne and Graz 1961.

JL=numbered papal letters in P. Jaffé, *Regesta pontificum Romanorum,* vol. 2. 2nd ed. Leipzig 1888. (L. stands for S. Loewenfeld, who revised Jaffé's original *Regesta* for the years 883–1198.)

Joanne, Paul. *Dictionnaire géographique et administratif de la France.* 7 vols. Paris 1890–1905.

Jordan, Rudolf. *Die Stellung des deutschen Episcopats im Kampf um die Universalmacht unter Friedrich I. bis zum Frieden von Venedig (1177).* Würzburg 1939.

Juncker, Josef. "Die Collectio Berolinensis." ZRG, Kan. Abt. 13 (1924) 284–426.

Knowles, David. *Colleagues=The Episcopal Colleagues of Archbishop Thomas Becket.* Cambridge 1951.

———. *Thomas Becket.* London 1970.

———, and R. Neville Hadcock. *Medieval Religious Houses, England and Wales.* New York 1971.

Kuttner, Stephan. "Alanus"="The Collection of Alanus: A Concordance of Its Two Recensions." *Rivista di storia del diritto italiano* 26 (1953) 37-53.

———. "Biberach"="The 'Extravagantes' of the Decretum in Biberach." *Bulletin of Medieval Canon Law*, n.s., 3 (1973) 61-71.

———. "Notes"="Notes on Manuscripts." *Traditio* 17 (1961) 533-42.

———. "Notes-Decretal Letters"="Notes on a Projected Corpus of Twelfth-Century Decretal Letters." *Traditio* 6 (1948) 345-51.

———. *Repertorium der Kanonistik (1140-1234)*. Studi e testi, 71. Vatican City 1937.

———, and Antonio García y García. "A New Eyewitness Account of the Fourth Lateran Council." *Traditio* 20 (1964) 115-78.

Labbe, Philippe, and Gabriel Cossart. *Sacrosancta concilia*. 17 vols. Paris 1671-72.

Le Bras, Gabriel. *Institutions ecclésiastiques de la Chrétienté médiévale* (= HE, 12). Paris 1959-64.

LTK=*Lexikon für Theologie und Kirche*. 11 vols. Freiburg 1957-67.

Luscombe, David E. *The School of Peter Abelard*. Cambridge Studies in Medieval Life and Thought, n.s., 14. Cambridge 1969.

Mansi, G. D. *Sacrorum conciliorum nova et amplissima collectio*. 31 vols. Florence and Venice 1759-98.

Mayr-Harting, Henry. "Hilary, Bishop of Chichester (1147-1169) and Henry II." *English Historical Review* 78 (1963) 209-24.

MGH SS=*Monumenta Germaniae historica, Scriptores*. 32 vols. Hannover 1826-1934.

Morey, Adrian, and C. N. L. Brooke. *Gilbert Foliot and His Letters*. Cambridge Studies in Medieval Life and Thought, n.s., 11. Cambridge 1965.

Munier, Charles. "L'*Ordo de celebrando concilio* wisigothique: Ses remaniements jusqu'au X$^e$ siècle." *Revue des sciences religieuses* 37 (1963) 250-71.

Munz, Peter. *Boso*=Introduction to *Boso's Life of Alexander III*. Trans. G. M. Ellis. Oxford 1973.

———. FB=*Frederick Barbarossa, A Study in Medieval Politics*. London 1969.

NCE=*New Catholic Encyclopedia*. 16 vols. New York 1967-74.

Ohnsorge, Werner. *Die Legaten Alexanders III. im ersten Jahrzehnt seines Pontifikats (1159-1169)*. Historische Studien, 175. Berlin 1928.

Pacaut, Marcel. "L. et A."="Louis VII et Alexandre III (1159-1180)." *Revue d'histoire de l'église de France* 39 (1953) 5-45.

———. *Louis VII et les élections épiscopales dans le royaume de France*. Paris 1957.

———. *Louis VII et son royaume*. Paris 1964.

PL=*Patrologiae cursus completus, Series Latina*. Edited by J. P. Migne. 221 vols. Paris 1844-64.

Poole, Austin Lane. *From Domesday Book to Magna Carta, 1087-1216*. Oxford History of England, 3. 2nd ed. Oxford 1958.

PUE=*Papsturkunden in England.* Edited by Walther Holtzmann. 3 vols. (Abhandlungen Göttingen, N.F., 25; 3.F., 14-15, 33). Berlin and Göttingen 1930-52.
PUF=*Papsturkunden in Frankreich.* Edited by Hermann Meinert and Johannes Ramackers. 6 vols. (Abh. Göttingen, 3.F., 3-4, 21, 23, 27, 35, 41). Berlin and Göttingen 1932-58.
PUFW=*Papsturkunden in Frankreich.* Edited by Wilhelm Wiederhold. 7 parts (Nachrichten Göttingen, phil.-hist. Kl., Beiheft). Berlin 1906-13.
PUP=*Papsturkunden in Portugal.* Edited by Carl Erdmann. Abh. Göttingen, N.F., 20:3. Berlin 1927.
PUS=*Papsturkunden in Spanien.* Edited by Paul Kehr. 2 vols. (Abh. Göttingen, N.F., 18:2, 22:1). Berlin 1926-28.

Quentin, Henri. *Jean-Dominique Mansi et les grandes collections conciliaires.* Paris 1900.

Reuter, Hermann F. *Geschichte Papst Alexanders des Dritten und der Kirche seiner Zeit,* vol. 1. Leipzig 1860.
RHGF=*Recueil des historiens des Gaules et de la France.* New ed. by Léopold Delisle. 19 vols. Paris 1869-80.
RS="Rolls Series"=*Rerum Britannicarum medii aevi scriptores.* 99 vols. London 1858-1911.

Schmale, Franz-Josef. "Friedrich I. und Ludwig VII. im Sommer des Jahres 1162." *Zeitschrift für bayerische Landesgeschichte* 31 (1968) 315-68.
———. *Studien zum Schisma des Jahres 1130.* Forschungen zur kirchlichen Rechtsgeschichte und zum Kirchenrecht, 3. Cologne and Graz 1961.
Scholz, Bernhard W. "The Canonization of Edward the Confessor." *Speculum* 36 (1961) 38-60.
Seckel, Emil. "Canonistische Quellen—Studien, I." *Deutsche Zeitschrift für Kirchenrecht,* ser. 3, 9 (1899-1900) 186-89 (Beilage: Die 12. falschen Canonen des Concils von Tours 1163).
Singer, Heinrich. *Neue Beiträge über die Dekretalensammlungen vor und nach Bernhard von Pavia.* Sitzungsberichte Vienna, 171:1. Vienna 1913.
Smalley, Beryl. *The Becket Conflict and the Schools.* Oxford 1973.
Somerville, Robert. "Council-Society"="The Council of Clermont (1095), and Latin Christian Society." *Archivum historiae pontificiae* 12 (1974) 55-90.
———. *Decreta*=*The Councils of Urban II, 1: Decreta Claromontensia.* Annuarium historiae conciliorum, Supp. 1. Amsterdam 1972.
———. "Pisa"="The Council of Pisa, 1135: A Re-examination of the Evidence for the Canons." *Speculum* 45 (1970) 98-114.
Southern, R. W. *Saint Anselm and His Biographer.* Cambridge 1963.
Stickler, Alfons. *Historia iuris canonici Latini, 1: Historia fontium.* Turin 1950.
Stones, E. L. G. *Anglo-Scottish Relations, 1174-1328.* London 1965.

Tangl, Georgine. *Die Teilnehmer an den allgemeinen Konzilien des Mittelalters.* Weimar 1922.

*Vita Alexandri*=Boso, VA, Duchesne, LP 2.397-446.

*Vita Hadriani IV*=Boso, VH, Duchesne, LP 2.338-97.

Von Giesebrecht, Wilhelm. *Geschichte der deutschen Kaiserzeit,* vol. 5:1. Leipzig 1880.

Von Heckel, Rudolf. "Die Dekretalensammlungen des Gilbertus und Alanus nach den Weingartenen Handschriften." ZRG, Kan. Abt. 29 (1940) 116-357.

Warren, Wilfred L. *Henry II.* Berkeley 1973.

Weigand, Rudolf. "Die Dekrethandschrift B 3515 des Spitalarchivs Biberach an der Riss." *Bulletin of Medieval Canon Law,* n.s., 2 (1972) 76-81.

X=*Liber extravagantium decretalium: see* Gregory IX.

ZRG, Kan. Abt.=*Zeitschrift der Savigny-Stiftung für Rechtsgeschichte,* Kanonistische Abteilung.

# Notes

## PREFACE

1. Foreville, *Latran* 411.

2. For this state of affairs, see inter al. Somerville, "Pisa," passim, especially the references in the notes on 98–100; Somerville, *Decreta* 6–19; Stephan Kuttner and Robert Somerville, "The So-Called Canons of Nîmes (1096)," *Tijdschrift voor Rechtsgeschiedenis* 38 (1970) 175–89.

3. Foreville, *Latran*. This study moves beyond Hefele-Leclercq by utilizing modern literature, but does not, unfortunately, present new manuscript research. See also the relevant pages of COD, for the twelfth-century Lateran councils; but even in this new edition of the canons problems remain: see Stephan Kuttner, "Brief Notes," *Traditio* 24 (1968) 505. For the notion of medieval "ecumenical" councils, see Fuhrmann, 680–90.

4. These notes cannot contain a detailed bibliography for the synods of this period. Hans-Georg Krause, *Das Papstwahldekret von 1059 und seine Rolle im Investiturstreit,* Studi Gregoriani, 7 (Rome 1960), for example, is concerned, obviously, with Pope Nicholas II's Lenten Synod in 1059.

5. See Robert Somerville, "The French Councils of Pope Urban II: Some Basic Considerations," *Annuarium historiae conciliorum* 2 (1970) 56–58.

6. E.g., HE 9:2.72–73.

7. E.g., Gabriel Le Bras et al., *L'âge classique, 1140–1378: Sources et théorie du droit.* Histoire du droit et des institutions de l'Église en Occident, 7 (Paris 1965) 145 n. 2, 159 n. 1.

8. A critical edition of the canons might alter such a history here and there: see the discussion below, 50. But the outline and most particulars will be constant, barring important new discoveries.

9. John T. Gilchrist, *The Church and Economic Activity in the Middle Ages* (London 1969) 17.

## 1. INTRODUCTION

1. JL 11207.

2. For the general history of the schism in 1159, the early years of Alexander III, etc., see HCH 4.52ff.; HE 9:2.5ff. The bibliography in the former (650ff.) is extensive, hence this study need not provide, either in footnotes or in the Bibliography, a general list of works on the period. Reuter, *Geschichte,* is old, but still necessary. Baldwin, *Alexander III,* presents a general

narrative of the pontificate, with space also devoted to Roland before his election as Alexander III; the work is useful as an introduction, but suffers occasionally from factual mistakes. Marcel Pacaut, *Alexandre III: Étude sur la conception du pouvoir pontifical dans sa pensée et dans son oeuvre,* L'Église et l'État au Moyen-Âge, 11 (Paris 1956), is a contribution to the history of ideas in the twelfth century, and contains useful sections. For papal chronologies and itineraries, JL is invaluable. The author has been unable to examine the D.Phil. thesis (Oxford, 1975), of Timothy Reuter (Exeter), titled *The Papal Schism, the Empire and the West, 1159–1169.* Ludwig Falkenstein, "Alexander III. und der Streit um die Doppelwahl in Châlons-sur-Marne (1162-1164)," *Deutsches Archiv* 32 (1976) 444-94, was published while the present work was in the press.

3. There is no modern monograph on this dual election: see HCH 4.57 n. 11; Munz, FB 205ff.

4. For Innocent II and the schism of 1130, see Schmale, *Studien;* Chodorow, 17ff. Reuter, 518ff., is useful for Alexander's trip to France.

5. *Vita Alexandri* 404. Cardinal Boso, the *Vita's* author, was not with Alexander at the time: Geisthardt, 67-68. For Boso generally, with recent bibliographies, see DBI 13.270-74; below, 20-21, 39 ff.

6. See Stephen of Rouen, RS 82:2.741, lines 921-22.

7. JL 10713.

8. JL 10644. See Janssen, 69; Pacaut, "L. et A.," passim.

9. Schmale, *Studien* 220ff.; Pacaut, "L. et A." 12.

10. RHGF 16.202, no. 10. See Heinemeyer, 157; Schmale, "Friedrich" 329ff.

11. The difficulties about this meeting are resolved by Cheney, "Recognition," especially 478ff. See also Peter Classen, "Das Konzil von Toulouse 1160: eine Fiktion," *Deutsches Archiv* 29 (1973) 220-23.

12. The trouble concerned a dispensation by Alexander's legates, allowing Louis's daughter and Henry's son, both under age, to marry: see Cheney, "Recognition" 493ff. The French princess was in Henry's custody, and the marriage had been arranged during the previous May. By obtaining this concession, Henry regained immediate possession of the Vexin and its castles, which were lost to Louis in the last years of King Stephen's reign, and which had been agreed upon as the princess's dowry. See Janssen, 66-69 (cf. Cheney, "Recognition" 480, 490-91); Pacaut, *Louis VII et son royaume* 72-73 (cf. Cheney, op. cit., passim), following his "L. et A." 16ff.; HE 9:2.61-62. Also of interest is Alexander's canonization of King Edward the Confessor in February 1161 (JL 10653 and 10654), a move strongly supported by Henry: see Scholz, passim.

13. Cheney, "Recognition" 496.

14. Hauck, 266-67.

15. For Louis's dealings with the imperial forces, see HE 9:2.69-71; Pacaut, "L. et A." 16-22; Heinemeyer, passim; Schmale, "Friedrich," passim.

16. JL 10757.

17. RS 82:4.215-16. For Robert's life and his work as a historian, see the editor's preface. According to Delisle, 2.vii-viii, he was on especially good terms with Henry II, hence could have known the king's movements. Romuald of Salerno's chronology is unreliable, but he reports the following (MGH SS 19.433): "Interea dum Alexander papa apud Salviniacum moraretur, primo rex Anglie ad eum veniens, ipsum cum universo regno in dominum et patrem recepit. Post hec rex Francie cum tota Gallicana ecclesia eum pro universali papa recipiens, honorifice Parisius usque deduxit." This seems to be a confused rendition of Louis's meeting with Alexander at Souvigny (post JL 10755), the papal meeting with Henry at Déols (see below, 4), and the trip which Alexander made to Paris early in 1163 (post JL 10814).

But Romuald continues: "Papa autem Alexander regem (*sic*) Francie et Anglie conveniens, pacem inter eos et concordiam reformavit." This could be a reference to the meeting described by Robert. For the editions of Romuald, see Hartmut Hoffmann, "Hugo Falcandus und Romuald von Salerno," *Deutsches Archiv* 23 (1967) 156ff.

18. Choisi: Eyton, 57; Chouzé: Richard Howlett, in the Preface to Stephen of Rouen, RS 82:2.lvi; Chouzy: Delisle, 1.342 n. 1; and for Coucy: Ilse Wolff, *Heinrich II. von England als Vasall Ludwigs VII. von Frankreich* (Breslau 1936) 7; HE 9:2.72; Baldwin, 63; HCH 4.59, all probably following Reuter, 227, where the reference to Robert in n. 1 should read VI, not VIII.

19. Here, and for what follows, see the place name entries in Joanne, *Dictionnaire*.

20. Carré de Busserolle, 1.287–89; Cottineau, 2.2299. See also Joanne, 2.982.

21. Ludovic Guignard, "Origines du bourg de Chouzy au point de vue Celtique, Gallo-Romain et Franc," *Association française pour l'avancement des sciences, Compte rendu de la 13ᵉ session, Blois, 1884,* 2 (1885) 708.

22. Adolphe L. Joanne, *Dictionnaire géographique, administratif . . . de la France* (Paris 1872) 565. This work, in two volumes, should be distinguished from that listed in the Bibliography, edited by Paul Joanne, which comprises seven volumes.

23. There is no entry for Chouzy-sur-Loire in the *Dictionnaire des communes* (Paris 1968). The Cisse is a tributary of the Loire, flowing close and often nearly parallel to the Loire. According to Joanne, 2.982, at Chouzy "la Cisse . . . sépare en deux bras dont l'un gagne aussitôt la rive dr. de la Loire, tandis que l'autre longe ce fl. jusque près de Tours."

24. Cottineau, 1.781, 1359–60; see also the bibliography given on 781 for the priory of St.-Martin.

25. Joanne, 2.983, reveals the existence of a village named Chouzy near La Chapelle-St.-Martin, which is located about four kilometers north of the Loire, northeast of Blois. See the detailed map of Loir-et-Cher, ibid., vol. 4, between 2220–21. It might be assumed that this was the site of the priory. But Cottineau, 1.781, placed the house in the canton of Herbault. As can be seen from Joanne's map, this also is true of Chouzy, sur-Cisse or sur-Loire. (See also under Joanne's description of Chouzy-sur-Cisse.) La Chapelle-St.-Martin, however, is in the canton of Mer: see Joanne, 2.855, and his map of Loir-et-Cher. Chouzy near La Chapelle is not on the Loire, and cannot be preferred, therefore, to Chouzy-sur-Loire as the site of the conference. The same holds for Chaussy-lès-Thoury, near Outarville, between Orléans and Étampes; Choussy, south of the Loire, north of the Forêt de Choussy; and Le Petit Chouzé, "près de la Loire," in the area of Chouzé: see Graesse et al., 1.382, s.v. *Calciacum;* Cottineau, 1.749; Carré de Busserolle, 1.287.

26. Ohnsorge, 55 n. 190. See also Munz, *Boso* 29–39.

27. He subscribed to JL 10759 and 10762. See Geisthardt, 68.

28. *Vita Alexandri* 407–08.

29. JL 10757. See the unfounded doubt about Henry's presence at Déols in Eyton, 57.

30. JL 10762.

31. Using only JL, the pope's movements between September 24 and October 10 are lost. But PUE 3.284–85, no. 142, adds new information. Alexander issued a letter on September 26 *apud sanctum Genulphum.* Holtzmann called attention to this unusual *datum,* and identified the place as St.-Genouph, a southwesterly suburb of Tours: see Carré de Busserolle, 3.183. But the matter is complicated. *Apud sanctum Genulphum* also designates the monastery of St.-Genou de l'Estrée, on the Indre, between Déols and Tours: see Cottineau, 2.2698; Graesse et al., 2.143, s.v. *s. Genulfus.* The papal party was substantial (see the subscriptions to the privilege in question), and would have moved slowly. To cover the more than 60 miles, as the crow flies, between Déols and Tours, within the period of time under discussion, would have been almost impossible: see Constable, 28–29, for a treatment of the speed of travel in the

twelfth century. It makes much more sense to locate Alexander at St.-Genou, about 17 miles from Déols, on September 26, and then to accept Boso's information that the pontiff reached Tours "about the time of the Feast of St. Michael," i.e., September 29: *Vita Alexandri* 408. From there, the pope and a party of advisers could have made their way up the Loire to Chouzy (about 38 miles), or, for that matter, down river to Chouzé (about 28 miles), conferred with Henry and Louis for a few days, and then returned to Tours by October 10.

32. R. W. Southern, *Western Society and the Church in the Middle Ages,* Pelican History of the Church, 2 (Harmondsworth 1970) 127.

33. *Vita Hadriani IV,* 391-92. See also Walter Heinemeyer, " 'beneficium—non feudum sed bonum factum': Der Streit auf dem Reichstag zu Besançon 1157," *Archiv für Diplomatik* 15 (1969) 191ff.; HCH 4.53; Robert Holtzmann, *Der Kaiser als Marschall des Papstes,* Schriften der Strassburger Wissenschaftlichen Gesellschaft in Heidelberg, N.F., 8 (Berlin and Leipzig 1928) 10.

34. Heinemeyer, 180ff.; HE 9:2.68-71. St.-Jean-de-Losne was in French territory: see Reuter, 527(d); JL 14470; post JL 14470. HE 9:2.71 placed the synod, for no apparent reason, at Dôle. See also the *Datum super Saonum fluvium* of the *Edictum de bannis regiis* of Frederick (1 September 1162): MGH, Leges, sect. 4, *Constitutiones et acta publica imperatorum et regum,* 1, ed. Ludwig Weiland (Hannover 1893) 308-09.

35. Saxo Grammaticus, MGH SS 29.114: "Post haec Regnaldus Coloniae urbis antistes religionis causam dicere adorsus, quanto iniuriae pondere Romani imperatoris aequitatem provincialium regum temeritas attemptaret, argumentando demonstrare pergebat. Nam si controversiam in eorum civitatibus de pontificatu ortam cesar suis suffragiis finire vellet, haud dubie id gravium iniuriarum loco ducerent, cum ipsi simile in urbe Roma perpetrare conentur." For the distinction between the emperor and "provincial kings," see also the anti-Hildebrandine letter written, probably by Cardinal Benno, toward the end of the eleventh century: MGH, *Libelli de lite,* 2 (Hannover 1892) 391, lines 37-39. See also Reuter, 530 (h); HE 9:2.71; Munz, FB 233-34.

36. Post JL 14428; post 14451; post 14476.

37. For Pavia, see HE 9:2.55-57; below, 7. Munz, FB 215, believes that Frederick at this point was truly impartial.

38. See below, 51-52, 54-55.

39. See the papal itineraries in JL, especially post JL 9197 and post 9280. JL offers a more accurate appraisal of the sources than either Mansi or Hefele-Leclercq. Foreville, *Latran* 101, has Eugene presiding at a synod in Trier, but see JL 9188. Detailed study is needed of the technical differences between an assembly of clerics and an actual "council": see, e.g., Häring, "Notes" 46-47.

40. For a general view of the papal councils from 1123 to 1215, especially those at the Lateran, see Foreville, *Latran* (although this work must be used carefully). For the synods between 1123 and 1130, and the sparse documentation for those gatherings, see in JL.

41. HCH 4.3.

42. For the schism in 1130, see the references in n. 4 above. For the Gregorian period generally, including the resolution of the Investiture Conflict, see HCH, vol. 3; HE, vol. 8.

43. For Innocent II's councils, see Somerville, "Pisa," to which the following can be added: Fidel Fita, "Actas del concilio de Clermont (18 noviembre 1130). Revisión crítica," *Boletín de la real academia de la historia* (Madrid) 4 (1884) 360-66; Girgensohn, passim; Robert Somerville, "The Canons of Reims (1131)," *Bulletin of Medieval Canon Law,* n.s., 5 (1975) 122-30.

44. For reservations about the influence of Lateran II, see C. R. Cheney, "The Numbering of the Lateran Councils of 1179 and 1215," in his *Medieval Texts and Studies* (Oxford 1973) 204ff. For Eugene III's conciliar activity, see Häring, "Notes" 39-45, and the same author's

"Die spanischen Teilnehmer am Konzil von Reims im März 1148," *Mediaeval Studies* 32 (1970) 159-71.

45. Carl Andresen, "History of the Medieval Councils in the West," in *The Councils of the Church*, ed. Hans Jochen Margull (Philadelphia 1966) 127-28 (trans. by Walter F. Bense of *Die ökumenischen Konzile der Christenheit*). For Arnold, see HCH 4.54, 98-99; HE 9:1.99-102. For an appeal in 1142 by Gerhoch of Reichersberg that a "general council" be convened to treat questions about *regalia,* see Benson, 308.

46. Chodorow, 17ff. The early sections of this book are a useful survey of scholarship, theories of dating, etc., concerning Gratian's work.

47. Stephan Kuttner, *Harmony from Dissonance: An Interpretation of Medieval Canon Law,* Wimmer Lecture, 10 (Latrobe, Pa. 1960) 26-28.

48. For decretal letters generally the literature is extensive. For an orientation, see Duggan, *Collections* (especially 121, for the increase in the volume of such letters); Gérard Fransen, *Les décrétales et les collections de décrétales,* Typologie des sources du moyen âge occidental, 2 (Turnhout 1972).

49. *De consideratione,* 1.3.4-1.4.5, *S. Bernardi opera,* ed. Jean Leclercq and Henri M. Rochais, 3 (Rome 1963) 399. The line about the Justinianic law, and the subsequent question, is a pun: "Et quidem quotidie perstrepunt in palatio leges, sed Iustiniani, non Domini. Iustene etiam istud?" For other pejorative comments by a mid-twelfth-century churchman about Roman Law, see Gerhoch of Reichersberg, *Letter to Pope Hadrian about the Novelties of the Day,* ed. Nicholas M. Häring, Pontifical Institute of Mediaeval Studies, Studies and Texts, 24 (Toronto 1974) 113-15. See also Chodorow, 61-62, 260-65 (but cf. the review by Robert L. Benson in *Speculum* 50 [1975] 100-101).

50. See Fuhrmann, 688, citing Tangl, 196ff.

51. See Reuter, 286-87; HE 9:2.71-72; Ohnsorge, 44-49, 154-60.

52. Heinemeyer, 166 n. 43; Ohnsorge, 44. See also Munz, FB 214ff.

53. *The Summa Parisiensis on the Decretum Gratiani,* ed. Terence P. McLaughlin, C.S.B. (Toronto 1952) 17: "Sciendum . . . quod concilium aliud generale quod fit praesente papa vel ejus legato vel alias ejus habita auctoritate, puta per litteras, et hoc solum potest canones constituere vel episcopum deponere." See also Gérard Fransen, "L'Ecclésiologie des conciles médiévaux," in *Le concile et les conciles* ([Gembloux] 1960) 125-41.

54. See Fuhrmann, 687.

55. *Ottonis et Rahewini gesta Friderici I. imperatoris,* ed. Georg Waitz and B. von Simson, MGH, Scriptores rerum Germanicarum in usum scholarum, 46 (Hannover and Leipzig 1912) 319: "Quamvis noverim officio ac dignitate imperii penes nos esse potestatem congregandorum conciliorum, presertim in tantis aecclesiae periculis—hoc enim et Constantinus et Theodosius necnon Iustinianus seu recentioris memoriae Karolus Magnus et Otto imperatores fecisse memorantur—, auctoritatem tamen diffiniendi huius maximi et summi negotii vestrae prudentiae vestraeque potestati committo." (In the recent edition of the *Gesta* by Franz-Josef Schmale—Ausgewählte Quellen zur Deutschen Geschichte des Mittelalters, Freiherr-vom-Stein-Gedächtnisausgabe, 17 [Berlin 1965]—this passage occurs at 660-62.) See also Alexander's comments about his summons to Pavia, in JL 10597.

56. Post JL 10718.

57. IP 7:1.225, no. 36 (JL 10719). For Henry and William, cardinal-priests of SS. Nereo e Achilleo and S. Pietro in Vincoli respectively, see Ohnsorge, 7, 43; Janssen, 61ff.; below, 14. The JL summary for this letter wrongly lists Toulouse for Toulon. I. P. Shaw, "The Ecclesiastical Policy of Henry II on the Continent, 1154-1189," *Church Quarterly Review* 151 (1950-51) 141 n. 18, makes the letter refer to Tours, not Montpellier.

58. IP 6:2.329, no. 28 (JL 10729).

59. Mansi, 21.1159-60; below, 54-55.
60. HCH 4.59.
61. Ohnsorge, 57, states, on the basis of JL 10772 and 10773, that Alexander conceived the idea at least by October 1162.
62. E. Martin-Chabot, "Deux bulles closes originales d'Alexandre III," *Mélanges d'archéologie et d'histoire*, École française de Rome 24 (1904) 65-74; PUS 1.381-82, no. 95. The fact that this is a *littere clause*, or "closed letter"—a document which could be read only after an irreparable removal of the fastening—might seem odd, since the contents do not appear to be remarkable. There is a good discussion of such letters in Martin-Chabot, and in Cheney and Cheney, xv. It is not easy to tell if a letter has been sealed thus unless evidence survives on the original. Since relatively few twelfth-century originals are extant, any comments about why Alexander employed the "closed" procedure in this case would be guesses. It is noteworthy, however, that another papal document from the same period, sent to the same area, also is "closed"—from Victor IV to Count Raymond of Provence and his wife, written in November 1161: see Paul Kehr, "Zur Geschichte Victors IV," *Neues Archiv* 46 (1929) 53-85.
63. Falkenstein, 117-18, 123-35, 148. See also Stephen of Rouen, RS 82:2.743, lines 961-62; Matthew Paris, RS 28:4:1.177. For papal subdeacons in the twelfth century, see Reinhard Elze, "Die päpstliche Kappelle im 12. und 13. Jahrhundert," ZRG, Kan. Abt. 36 (1950) 153-71, especially 161ff.
64. Pacaut, "L. et A." 22-23; Pacaut, *Louis VII et les élections* 64-65; Warren, 451-52.
65. Avrom Saltman, *Theobald, Archbishop of Canterbury*, University of London Historical Studies, 2 (London 1956) 25ff.; Warren, 452.
66. Falkenstein, 117.
67. RS 68:1.310.
68. Duggan, "Conquest" 92.
69. See Warren, passim, especially 426-27, 477; Smalley, 119-20; Mayr-Harting, 210-11.
70. JL 10834. Warren, 452, places this letter, without explanation, after the council.
71. Eyton, 58-59, shows Henry in England in the early months of 1163, and notes a gathering in London on March 3, plus an impressive list of English prelates as assessors in a suit at Westminster on March 8, between Robert of Lincoln and Robert of St. Albans. Mayr-Harting, 216 n. 6, with the reference to Hearne, *Liber Niger* 41-42, is citing JL 10834.
72. See HL 5:2.964; Pacaut, "L. et A." 23 n. 67; HE 9:2.72.
73. Ordericus Vitalis, *Historia ecclesiastica*, 12.21, ed. Auguste Le Prevost, 4 (Paris 1852) 373, for Reims (see Hugh the Chantor regarding a seating problem at this synod: *The History of the Church of York, 1066-1127*, ed. and trans. Charles Johnson [London 1961] 74). See William Stubbs, *Select Charters . . .* , 9th ed. revised by H. W. C. Davis (Oxford 1966) 163ff., for Clarendon. See also Poole, 184, 194, 205; Warren, 452. For Ordericus and King Henry see Roger D. Ray, "Orderic Vitalis on Henry I: Theocratic Ideology and Didactic Narrative," in *Contemporary Reflections on the Medieval Christian Tradition: Essays in Honor of Ray C. Petry*, ed. George H. Shriver (Durham, N.C. 1974) 119-34.
74. RS 28:4:1.177-78. See also Richard Vaughan, *Matthew Paris*, Cambridge Studies in Medieval Life and Thought, n.s., 6 (Cambridge 1958) 182ff.
75. See Foreville, *Église* 115.
76. See Warren, 452.
77. Above, 2.
78. Smalley, 159.
79. JL 10773. See Ohnsorge, 50.
80. It was a common medieval practice for important messages to be delivered orally rather than committed to writing. The letters carried by a messenger might be little more than intro-

ductions. For an indispensable discussion of this and other matters relating to medieval letters, see Constable, 25ff.

81. JL 10772. See Pacaut, *Louis VII et les élections* 50-51.

82. See Janssen, 81.

83. JL 10789.

84. See n. 80 above. The verb used is *intimare,* perhaps implying a secretive character to the dealings.

85. Post JL 10814.

86. RHGF 16.47. See Achille Luchaire, *Études sur les actes de Louis VII* (Paris 1885) 251. For what follows about St.-Martin's and the history of Tours, see Edgard-Raphaël Vaucelle, *La Collégiale de Saint-Martin de Tours . . . (397-1328)* (Paris 1908) 80, 273, 275, 279-80, 441.

87. See Robert Somerville, "The French Councils of Pope Urban II: Some Basic Considerations," *Annuarium historiae conciliorum* 2 (1970) 65; Häring, "Notes" 39, 43.

88. Somerville, "French Councils," passim; post JL 5620; Mansi, 20.925.

89. Francis Salet, *La cathédrale de Tours* (Paris 1949) 5-7, and "La cathédrale de Tours," *Congrès archéologique de France* 106 (1949) 30-32.

90. See ibid., for a fire in the cathedral soon after the council. For the date and church, see *Vita Alexandri* 408; the letter to Alphonso of Aragon (n. 62 above); Reuter, 546 (a); post JL 10859. Ralph of Diceto, RS 68:1.310, and Roger Wendover and Matthew Paris, RS 84:1.26, and 44:1.321, respectively, incorrectly dated the council May 21. Baldwin, 64, has the assembly opening on 19 September 1163.

## 2. CONCILIAR ORGANIZATION, I: THE SERMONS

1. See Somerville, *Decreta* 23ff.; Foreville, *Latran,* passim; Foreville, "Procédure et débats dans les conciles médiévaux du Latran (1123-1215)," *Rivista di storia della Chiesa in Italia* 19 (1965) 21-37; Cheney, "Problems."

2. Foreville, *Latran* 195-99 (see also 136-37); idem, "Procédure" (n. 1 above) 29. This text is edited in Michel Andrieu, *Le pontifical romain au moyen-âge,* 1: *Le pontifical romain du XII^e siècle,* Studi e testi, 86 (Vatican City 1938) 255ff. See also the editor's introduction, ibid.; Munier, passim.

3. Kuttner-García, "Lateran."

4. For an analogous problem in a council at St. Peter's in 1099, see Somerville, *Decreta* 24; and for the same situation at Tours, see below, 15.

5. See Le Bras, 334 n. 6.

6. Smalley, 186ff. Richard Howlett, in RS 82:2, is the edition used. For others, see August Potthast, *Biblioteca historica medii aevi,* 2 (2nd ed. Berlin 1896) 1034.

7. Howlett, RS 82:2.lxxxvii.

8. Ibid., ix-x.

9. Ibid., 742-52 (this is in Book III of the work), for the account; 742 n. 1, for Reims.

10. Ibid., vii ff. This is not the only papal council whose location Stephen seems to have confused. Due to a misread source, Innocent II's 1131 council is placed in Paris rather than Reims: ibid., 650, line 1536; see also xxiv-xxv.

11. Smalley, 112.

12. RS 82:2.744, lines 997-98.

13. Smalley, 187-88, 155.

14. RS 82:2.752, lines 1227-28. See also JL 11256; Munz, *Boso* 19-20.

15. RS 82:2.743, line 965. Regarding bribery at Tours by the abbot of Bury St. Edmunds, see Matthew Paris, RS 28:4:1.178.

16. RS 82:2.751, line 1213.

17. Ibid., 743, lines 963-64. See William E. Lunt, *Financial Relations of the Papacy with England to 1327,* Mediaeval Academy of America Publications, 33 (Cambridge, Mass. 1939) 514; Geisthardt, 78.

18. RS 82:2.743, lines 973-74. See also Matthew Paris, RS 28:4:1.178, lines 27ff., for gifts brought to the pope and cardinals at Tours.

19. RS 82:2.743, lines 987ff. Stephen also devotes attention to the rivalry at Tours between Archbishops Roger of York and Thomas Becket of Canterbury. In so doing, he recounts Roger's verbal activity on his own behalf: "He made everything resound with a great whirl of words" (*turbine verborum,* ibid., 746, line 1058). This activity concerned a special *causa* at the synod (the *Draco* uses that very word, ibid., 744, lines 1007, 1015), which was protracted for several days, and undoubtedly involved several discourses. Stephen does not indicate how many; and he distinguishes the opening sermon from the *causarum turba* which followed *hos post sermones,* and into which the York-Canterbury affair belongs: ibid., line 1005. For the York-Canterbury contest at Tours, see below in Chapter 4.

20. It is overwhelmingly probable that these words (RS 82:2.746-51) are Stephen's invention and, as such, have nothing to do with Tours. They are, nonetheless, valuable at the very least as one writer's opinion about aspects of the schism. See Chapter 4, n. 22. Stephen treats this final address of Alexander as a special event which terminated the assembly.

21. Reuter, 287 n. 1, quoted and utilized a passage out of Mansi, 21.1186, included there among the *Acta concilii Turonensis e variis auctoribus excerpta a Severino Binio,* and attributed to a *Robertus* who was at Tours. This text, asserting that the initial conciliar event was a speech by Alexander recounting his claims and anathematizing Victor and his accomplices, came into Binius's work from Baronius (Baronius, 19.209; Binius 3:2.534), and thus traversed the various conciliar collections: see n. 47 below. It is not a direct quotation but a paraphrase, as indicated by the type in these printings. Robert of Torigny comes to mind at once. He was at Tours (see below, 29), but his major work provides only the briefest account of the synod (RS 82:4.219), and gives none of the details of the Baronius-Binius-Mansi text; it could however be the starting point for an editorially embellished description, since it does note the condemnations. None of Robert's other works is applicable, nor is his contemporary Robert of Auxerre: see MGH SS 26.238. The matter remains unresolved, with a strong possibility that Baronius distorted the short statement noted in RS 82:4.

22. The evidence adduced pro and con on this issue (Foreville, *Église* 242, 277; Poole, 197; Smalley, 112) is circumstantial or anachronistic.

23. For Bishop Hilary of Chichester in an analogous verbal predicament at a later date, see Alan of Tewkesbury, RS 67:2.338-39. See also Knowles, *Colleagues* 64.

24. See above, 2.

25. Cheney, "Recognition" 482-85. See also Janssen, 61-78, especially 65-68.

26. Cheney, "Recognition," especially 485-86, 495-96.

27. See above, n. 12 of Chapter 1, especially Janssen.

28. Pacaut, *Louis VII et les élections* 151.

29. RS 82:2.744, lines 999-1000.

30. Giles, 2-3.

31. See below, 16.

32. RS 82:2.744, lines 1001-02.

33. See Reuter, 293; Le Bras, 336. The council lasted no more than eleven days, for it was over on May 29: GP 1.30, no. 96 (JL 10869). At one point (Mansi, 21.1170), Arnulf's written

version of his sermon addresses bishops directly. If more information were available about conciliar procedure, and if stylistic adjustments on Arnulf's part between the spoken and published versions of his text could be discounted, this might give a clue about when the discourse was delivered: see the remarks above, 12, about the separate seating of bishops and abbots at Lateran IV.

34. Nicolas Travers (d. 1750), *Histoire civile, politique et religieuse de la ville et du comté de Nantes,* 1 (Nantes 1836) 289, declared, but without a proper citation, that Bishop Bernard of Nantes spoke at Tours; see DHGE 8.701, for reservations about this. For Travers, see now Avril, "La province de Tours."

35. RS 82:2.744, lines 997-98.

36. Knowles, *Colleagues* 58.

37. Barlow, xxiv-xxv. For twelfth-century estimates of Arnulf, see ibid., xv, xx n. 7, xxv-xxvii, xxxi.

38. Smalley, 166.

39. Barlow, xiii ff.

40. Ibid., xl; Smalley, 141.

41. Barlow, xxi.

42. Giles, 1-2.

43. Pacaut, *Louis VII et les élections* 150.

44. Reuter, 546-47 (b), also points out some minor differences, but not all, between the versions.

45. Barlow, lxxxvii, lxvi ff. The sermon's presence in this edition (not seen by the author) can be assumed on the basis of Baronius's comment (see next note) about finding it in the recently printed collection of Arnulf's letters.

46. Baronius, 19.202ff. See also Barlow, lxxxvii; *Catalogue général des livres imprimés de la Bibliothèque nationale,* 84 (Paris 1925) 462-66. The author has examined the text in *Magna bibliotheca veterum patrum,* 3 (Paris 1644) 573ff.

47. Binius, 3:2.530-33; Mansi, 21.1167ff. For the progression of texts into and through the early modern conciliar editions to Mansi, see Somerville, *Decreta* 6ff.

48. Giles, 2-16.

49. Ibid., xi-xii; Barlow, lxxvii-lxxviii, lxvi ff.

50. Barlow, lxii. See also Reuter, 287.

51. Giles, 2.

52. The sermon's contents are summarized by Reuter, 287-88; HL 5:2.969-70. All citations here are to the text in Mansi. The present passage is 21.1169-70.

53. See Reuter, 287.

54. For *sacramentum unitatis,* see Boso, *Vita Alexandri* 411. See also JL 14445, from Victor IV.

55. Mansi, 21.1170.

56. Ibid.

57. Ibid.

58. Mansi, 21.1170, writes *obtinebimus.* Giles, 6, has *obtinemus,* as does Baronius, 19.204, which is the source of the text which entered the stream of conciliar compilations: see above, nn. 46, 47. See also the *obtinemus* in Binius, 3:2.531; Labbe-Cossart, 10.1415; Hardouin, 6:2.2591.

59. Mansi 21.1170. See also the passage quoted from Arnulf by Reuter, 288 n. 1, which is found in Mansi, 21.1171 (where it begins *Nos,* not *Vos* as in Reuter's quotation).

60. Mansi 21.1170-71. See the different interpretation of this verse given by Peter the Venerable, PL 189.573ff.

61. For the number of abbots, see below, 20-21; 29ff.

62. Reuter, 286-87; HL 5:2.970.

63. RS 82:2.751. See above, 13-14.

64. See n. 20 above. For other condemnations by popes, perhaps at the end of councils, see Eadmer, RS 81.106ff., and William of Malmesbury, RS 52.100 (Urban II at Bari, 1098); Eadmer, RS 81.114 (Urban II at Rome, 1099); Hesso, MGH SS 12.428, and Ordericus Vitalis, ed. Auguste Le Prevost, 4 (Paris 1852) 391 (Calixtus II at Reims, 1119). See also Somerville, *Decreta* 24ff.

65. See below, 64ff., for Frederick.

66. See above, 8.

67. Reuter, 286.

## 3. CONCILIAR ORGANIZATION, II: THE PARTICIPANTS

1. Above, 8-9.

2. *S. Anselmi . . . opera omnia,* ed. F. S. Schmitt, 4 (Edinburgh 1949) 119-21. See also ibid., 5 (Edinburgh 1951) 258-59.

3. See HE 8.329-30; HL 5:1.461-63; Somerville, *Decreta* 24-25; *The Life of St. Anselm by Eadmer,* ed. and trans. R. W. Southern (London 1962) 115.

4. LTK 4.1140, for Geoffrey; Gams, 489, for Ulger. For Ulger see also Brooke-Morey-Brooke, 65 n. 2—a reference kindly passed to the author by Professor C. N. L. Brooke, University of London.

5. Somerville, *Decreta* 122-23.

6. Ibid., 139-40, for instances of the occurrence of this decree. See also RHGF 14.736 n. (b); 15.19 nn. (c and d).

7. PL 157.119.

8. For Geoffrey as a forger, see Somerville, "Council-Society" 89; Somerville, *Decreta* 140 n. 9. Add to the references given in those places *Histoire littéraire de la France,* 11 (Paris 1759) 177-208.

9. Cheney, "Problems" 168. See also Somerville, *Decreta* 24 n. 25; and relative to the *ordo* noted there, see Munier, passim; Cheney, "Problems" 169 n. 8; C. R. Cheney, "Legislation of the Medieval English Church, Part I," *English Historical Review* 50 (1935) 208-09. Further, see the interesting remarks by John of Salisbury, *Historia pontificalis,* ed. Marjorie Chibnall (London 1962) 8-10, on the promulgation and interpretation of canons from Reims, 1148.

10. Fragments of a detailed attendance list survive for Alexander III's Lateran Council of 1179, probably based on a census made at the synod by William of Tyre: see William of Tyre, *Historia rerum in partibus transmarinis gestarum,* 21.26, in *Recueil des historiens des croisades: Historiens occidentaux,* 1:2 (Paris 1844) 1051. See also Foreville, *Latran* 139-40, 387-90; Tangl, 212; COD 181 n. 4. The extant versions are in Mansi, 22.213ff. (repeated at 239ff.) and 458ff., the latter being more complete. Foreville, *Latran* 387ff., gives a French translation of what seems to be a composite of these two texts. For eleventh- and twelfth-century attendance reports prior to 1179, see nn. 29, 30 below.

11. RHGF 14.98. See also Somerville, "Council-Society" 64-65.

12. MGH, Leges, sect. 4, *Constitutiones et acta publica imperatorum et regum,* 1, ed. Ludwig Weiland (Hannover 1893) 570-73. See also Otto Schumann, "Zu den Teilnehmerlisten des Protokolls über den letzten Tag des Laterankonzils von 1112," *Neues Archiv* 35 (1910) 789-91.

13. Weiland, *Constitutiones* (n. 12 above) 572.

14. See HCH 3.396-97; HE 8.356-71.

15. Tangl, 189.
16. Girgensohn, 1073.
17. *Vita Alexandri* 408.
18. Geisthardt, 63, 77ff.; Duchesne, LP 2.xl–xliii. Boso can be placed with certainty in the papal party on 29 April 1163 (JL 10857, subscription), and he was at Tours on June 5 (IP 3.39-40, no. 4 [JL 10875], subscription). It is inconceivable, barring illness, that he would have missed the synod: see DBI 13.272.
19. The material about Tours presented by Boso could have been copied from the official protocol. For Boso's access to papal registers, see Duchesne, LP 2.xli; DBI 13.273.
20. MGH SS 26.445.
21. Häring, "John" 257.
22. RS 68:1.310. See also Barrow, *Malcolm* 17.
23. MGH SS 19.433.
24. *Chroniques des églises d'Anjou,* ed. Paul Marchegay and Émile Mabille (Paris 1869) 40.
25. MGH SS 26.148-49. (Professor C. N. L. Brooke, University of London, has pointed out that this work has recently been reedited by R. B. C. Huygens, *Monumenta Vizeliacensia,* Corpus Christianorum, Cont. med., 42 [Turnhout 1976], with the passages here cited at 528-29.) Foreville, *Latran* 119, gives a list of regions from which clerics came to Tours, but offers no reference. She probably is following Reuter, 286 (see also HL 5:2.969), who based his comments on Hugh. Hugh does not say that prelates from the Latin Orient were at Tours, but only that Sardinia, Sicily with all of Calabria, the oriental Church, and Spain each *devotum obedientiae caput humiliter Alexandro catholico papae subdidit.* How that occurred is unspecified.
26. Hugh mentions Cluny. For the schism's effect on abbatial government there, see HE 9:2.62; DHGE 13.73-74; Munz, FB 223 n. 5; Dieter Hägermann, "Ein Brief Erzbischof Christians I. von Mainz an die Mönche von Cluny," *Archiv für Diplomatik* 15 (1969) 237-50; below, 64.
27. GP 1.30, no. 96 (JL 10869).
28. ". . . magnificum et sollempne concilium . . . celebravimus, ut nullus unquam predecessorum nostrorum a xl retro annis maius vel sollemnius, sicut antiquiores, qui consueverunt in ultramontanis partibus interesse conciliis, protestantur, celebrare se noscatur."
29. See Girgensohn, passim. There is no attendance list extant for Lateran II: see Tangl, 198, 205-10; Foreville, *Latran* 78-79.
30. See HL 5:1.687, 694, 823; ante JL 7489; the discussion of Pisa, above.
31. Felix Liebermann, *Ungedruckte Anglo-Normannische Geschichtsquellen* (Strasbourg 1879) 84-96, discussed this manuscript, and edited the *Annales.* Much of the following section is dependent on his observations. See also E. W. Williamson, *The Letters of Osbert of Clare* (London 1929) 33; N. R. Ker, *Medieval Libraries of Great Britain,* Royal Historical Society Guides and Handbooks, 3 (London 1964) 51.
32. PUE 1.92. See also Williamson (n. 31 above), loc. cit.
33. This is noteworthy, but should not be overstressed, since, as will be considered, it is unclear how the list was arranged.
34. For Hereford and Carlisle, see Sir F. M. Powicke and E. B. Fryde, *Handbook of British Chronology,* Royal Historical Society Guides and Handbooks, 2 (London 1961) 229; *Fasti* 19; Barrow, *Malcolm* 16. For additional evidence of this sort, consider the fact that the archbishop of Auch, who died on the way to Tours (Engel, 98), does not appear in the attendance list under discussion.
35. RS 68:1.310. See also Roger Wendover, RS 84:1.26.
36. See the following chapter for the bishop of Dunkeld, Scotland, at the council.
37. *Fasti* 99.

38. François M. Duine, *La métropole de Bretagne,* La Bretagne et les pays celtiques, 2ᵉ sér. in 8°, 12 (Paris 1916) 130.

39. JL 10671.

40. For the obscurity of many aspects of the twelfth-century Spanish Church, see D. W. Lomax, "Don Ramón, Bishop of Palencia (1148-84)," in *Homenaje a Jaime Vicens Vives,* 1 (Barcelona 1965) 279-91.

41. For Santiago, see Antonio López-Ferreiro, *Historia de la santa A. M. Iglesia de Santiago de Compostela,* 4 (Santiago 1901) 270-81.

42. See above, 20.

43. See above, 21.

44. *Chronica minora saec. IV, V, VI, VII,* ed. Theodor Mommsen, MGH, Auctores antiquissimi, 9:1 (Berlin 1892) 552-612.

45. The suffragan composition of ecclesiastical provinces in France in the twelfth century can be derived from Robert Holtzmann, *Französische Verfassungsgeschichte,* Handbuch der mittelalterlichen und neueren Geschichte, 3 (Munich and Berlin 1910) 140-41, 289-90, used together with works such as Conrad Eubel, *Hierarchia catholica medii aevi,* 1 (Münster 1913), especially 540ff., Gams, DHGE, and LTK.

46. This is on the basis of those works cited in the previous note.

47. Mommsen (n. 44 above) 610.

48. DBI 2.11-12; for the date, see Nicholas M. Häring, "Texts concerning Gilbert of Poitiers," *Archives d'histoire doctrinale et littéraire du moyen-âge* 37 (1971) 177.

49. See Michel Andrieu, *Les Ordines Romani du haut moyen-âge,* 1: *Les manuscrits,* Spicilegium sacrum Lovaniense, Études et documents, 11 (Louvain 1931) 317-18, for the title of this work, which was known traditionally as *Gesta pauperis scholaris.* See also *Repertorium fontium historiae medii aevi,* 2 (Rome 1967) 177. This text is edited in Fabre-Duchesne, 2.97-104; see also ibid., 1.43-56.

50. Fabre-Duchesne, 1.56; see also 5-7.

51. See above, 8.

52. See above, 21.

53. See JL 10882. See also Barrow, *Malcolm* 17; but compare the discussion below, 29-30, about the quality of evidence of this sort.

54. Girgensohn, 1082. See also Matthew Paris, RS 28:4:1.178, lines 27-28. For the attendance lists extant for the Lateran councils of 1179 and 1215, see Tangl, 210ff. The following figures for Irish and Scottish bishops can be found: Lateran 1179 (see Mansi, 22.468)— 7 Irish prelates (out of 38 dioceses, on the basis of the listing from 1192 in the *Liber censuum* [Fabre-Duchesne, 1.232-34]), and 1 Scot, but from the references below in this note, 2 additional Scottish bishops can be assumed (see Foreville, *Latran* 390), for a total of 3 (out of 10 dioceses, on the basis of the *Fasti Scot.,* excluding the dioceses of the Isles and of Orkney, which from 1153 were under the metropolitan authority of Trondheim: ibid., 197, 247); Lateran 1215 (see Jakob Werner, "Nachlese aus Zürcher Handschriften, I," *Neues Archiv* 31 [1906] 577-93)—17 Irishmen (from 38 dioceses, still using the *Liber censuum*), and 4 Scots (from 10 dioceses, substituting now the recently created see of Argyll for Galloway, which remained under the jurisdiction of York after the exemption granted to the Scottish Church in 1192: *Fasti Scot.* 26, 128). See also below, 33, for the exemption.

The *Annales Stadenses* (MGH SS 16.349) relate interesting information about Scottish and Irish participants at Lateran III in 1179: one Scottish bishop came with a single horse, and another on foot with one companion. An Irish bishop at the same synod is reported to have described his resources as three milk cows, which were replaced periodically by his parishioners. See also Charles Burns, "Two Scottish Bishops Consecrated at the Third Lateran Council," *Innes Review* 11 (1960) 68; *Fasti Scot.* 39, 75 (but the reference given in the latter place—

Alan O. Anderson, *Early Sources of Scottish History, A.D. 500 to 1286,* 2 [Edinburgh and London 1922] 300—mistranslates the *Annales*); Alexander R. MacEwen, *A History of the Church in Scotland,* 1 (London and New York 1913) 229. The story also is included by Hubert Jedin, *Ecumenical Councils of the Catholic Church* (New York 1960) 76 (trans. by Ernest Graf).

55. RS 21:3.155. See also James C. Davies, *Episcopal Acts and Cognate Documents Relating to Welsh Dioceses, 1066–1272,* Historical Society of the Church in Wales, 1-4 (Cardiff 1946-48) 1.273.

56. Davies (n. 55 above) 2.417.

57. Above, 21. See also JL 10876 (Davies [n. 55 above] 1.273), for Sherborne in the diocese of St. Davids, issued after the council, and perhaps indicating participation from this area. But note the caveat regarding this sort of evidence, below, 29-30.

58. A word is needed about Bishop Albert of Freising. As a pilgrim journeying to Compostela, he probably passed through Tours at about the time of the synod. Engel, 90-100, especially 96-97, discussed the question of Albert's participation, and concluded that he was not among the council fathers. Classen, 211, regarded Albert as a conciliar participant, and referred to Engel, "dessen Ausführungen jedoch willkürliche Kombinationen und chronologische Fehler enthalten." The evidence, which is presented by Engel, especially at 96 n. 23, is inconclusive; but it makes sense to imagine that if Albert reached Tours during the time of the synod, he would have passed through quickly, fearing imperial outrage if he were to remain. (For pressures brought to bear in 1165 against Albert, by Frederick Barbarossa, see Benson, 246 n. 58 and 286.) In light of the negligible German attendance at the council, it is interesting to speculate about the means of delivery of GP 1.30, no. 96 (JL 10869), to Salzburg (see above, 21). The letter is dated after the synod. Could it have been entrusted to Albert, and if so, when and where?

59. Above, n. 10.

60. For a negative opinion about Hilary's attendance, see Mayr-Harting, 216-17 n. 6, repeated in the same author's *Diocesis Cicestrensis: The Acta of the Bishops of Chichester, 1075-1207,* The Canterbury and York Society, 56, Part 130 (Torquay 1964) 58 n. 4.

61. See, e.g., Somerville, *Decreta* 29-30.

62. RS 84:2.156. Roger had been speaking of all who came to Lateran IV—bishops, abbots, priors, etc. He then remarked, "When everyone had been gathered in the aforesaid place [the Lateran basilica], *juxta morem conciliorum generalium in suis ordinibus singulis collocatis.* . . ." This could mean, presumably, that all members of a particular *ordo,* i.e. bishops, abbots, etc., sat together, or it could mean that an unspecified, traditional procedure was being used, so that "everyone was in his proper place." The latter reading seems preferable.

63. See Gratian, D. 17, [c. 7], and the *dictum* following; Munier, 265; Richard Kay, "An Eyewitness Account of the 1225 Council of Bourges," *Studia Gratiana* 12 (1967) 72, for a thirteenth-century legatine council. The second reference in Gratian also addresses the problem of whether the consecration should be understood *ad ecclesias,* or *ad personas,* and opts for the latter. Thus a transferred bishop retains his seniority *ad personam,* and is not reduced in status by his new situation *ad ecclesiam.*

64. Cheney, "Problems" 169-70; and especially C. N. L. Brooke, "Archbishop Lanfranc, the English Bishops, and the Council of London of 1075," *Studia Gratiana* 12 (1967) 39-59.

65. Mansi, 20.451. See also Brooke (n. 64 above) 47. The text and the sources for this council will be presented and evaluated in the forthcoming volume of *Councils and Synods,* ed. Martin Brett, C. N. L. Brooke, and Dorothy Whitelock.

66. See Brooke (n. 64 above) 47-48, for Worcester as an exception to this rule in 1075.

67. This letter was unknown to JL. It survives in the York register, and is edited in RS 71:3.72.

68. LTK 6.960, 2.789, 6.974, 9.596.

69. Ibid., 6.1294, 8.236, 10.724, 10.407.

70. See the following chapter.

71. See, e.g., Girgensohn, 1075; Kuttner-García, 124 (cf. 127); Somerville, *Decreta* 29.

72. Girgensohn, passim.

73. Excluding the archbishop-elect of Compostela; see above, 23.

74. Gams, *Series episcoporum;* Pacaut, *Louis VII et les élections.*

75. Above, 25.

76. Graesse et al., 1.182.

77. Ibid., 2.267, s.v. *s. Iacobus de Compostella.*

78. Professor John Mundy has pointed out that in later medieval documents, "7" and "9" occur interchangeably at the end of place identifications.

79. This striking form is an additional example of the near illiteracy of the scribe. See also nn. 80, 84.

80. Professor Mundy has suggested that this form probably refers to Couserans. See Graesse et al., 2.387, s. v. *Licerium Conseranum;* LTK 3.79. The other, less likely, possibility is Comminges: see Graesse et al., 2.424, s. v. *Lugdunum Convenarum.*

81. Graesse et al., 3.497, s. v. *Toletum;* but ibid. indicates that *Tolletanensis* is possible.

82. For Zamora as a suffragan of Braga, see D. Marsilla, "Disputas diocesanas entre Toledo, Braga y Compostela en los siglos XII al XV," *Anthologica annua* 3 (1955) 91–113, especially 102–03.

83. There was a schism in the church at Pamplona at the time of the council. Robert of Torigny remarked about it (RS 82:4.119-20), in terms of Alexander's decision at Tours to set aside the conflicting candidates and have a third chosen. See José Gavira Martín, *Estudios sobre la iglesia española medieval: Episcopologios de sedes navarro-aragonesas durante los siglos XI y XII* (Madrid 1929) 93–94 (he neglects Robert's testimony); J. Goñi Gaztambide, "Los obispos de Pamplona del siglo XII," *Anthologica annua* 13 (1965) 279–82; *Diccionario de historia eclesiástica de España,* ed. Quintín Aldea Vaquero et al., 3 (Madrid 1973) 1875. Since the attendance compilation mentions only an *episcopus Pampilenensis,* it is impossible to say anything more than that the divided see was represented.

84. This is an unusual form for Béziers (Graesse et al., 1.201, s. v. *Baeterrae*), but Béziers is the only possibility.

85. See above, 26, for this grouping.

86. Above, 21.

87. E.g., Girgensohn, 1081.

88. See Chapter 2, n. 33.

89. See above, 20.

90. JL 10871.

91. MGH SS 25.806. See also PL 200.251 n. 95.

92. Above, 9; above, n. 26; RS 82:4.298. See also the Mont St.-Michel *Annales,* ed. Delisle, 2.228. LTK 8.1343, followed by NCE 12.536, specifies that Alexander "invited" Robert to Tours, but offers no source.

93. See Matthew Paris, RS 28:4:1.179, for Abbot Robert of St. Albans hurrying home following the council at Tours, and leaving a deputy to solicit a desired privilege: PUE 3.290, no. 148. See also Somerville, "Council-Society" 83.

94. See n. 58 above, for speculation of this sort concerning Bishop Albert of Freising.

95. For the Göttingen *Papsturkunden-Pontificia* project, see Leo Santifaller, *Neuere Editionen mittelalterlicher Königs- und Papsturkunden: Eine Übersicht,* Österreichische Akademie der Wissenschaften: Mitteilungen der Wiener Diplomata-Abteilung der MGH, 6 (Vienna 1958) 63ff.

96. Only letters which can be dated precisely are included, but these chronological boundaries are not foolproof. See, for example, JL 10905, dated July 11, which is treated below, Chapter 6, n. 18. PUE 3.285-86, no. 143, to Southwick (Augustinian, Knowles-Hadcock, 174), is omitted, although issued at Tours, since it can be dated no more accurately than 10 October 1162-18 June 1163, excluding the period in February-April when Alexander was in Paris. IP 5.484, no. 1 (JL 10895), dated 15 June 1163, to the so-called *Congregatio clericorum* at Piacenza, also is excluded, but it can be mentioned as one of two letters from Alexander III during this period directed to Italy (see IP 3.39-40, no. 4 [JL 10875], to S. Salvi in Florence).

97. See also Rudolf Hiestand, *Vorarbeiten zum Oriens pontificius*, 1: *Papsturkunden für Templer und Johanniter*, Abhandlungen Göttingen, 3. Folge, 77 (Göttingen 1972) 245-46, nos. 43-45; PUS 1.386, no. 100; JL 10897 (cf. PUS 1.388-89, no. 103).

98. See also JL 10865; 10866 (cf. PUF 3.110-11, nos. 54-55).

99. See also JL 10898.

100. Cf. PUFW 2 (1906) 46, no. 22.

101. See n. 93 above.

102. Cf. PUFW 7 (1913) 110-11, no. 62.

103. Cf. ibid., 5 (1910) 74-77, no. 43.

104. Above, 20.

105. For such subscriptions generally, see Cheney and Cheney, xiii; Bruno Katterbach, O.F.M., and Wilhelm M. Peitz, S.J., "Die Unterschriften der Päpste und Kardinäle in den 'Bullae maiores' vom 11. bis 14. Jhdt.," in *Miscellanea Francesco Ehrle*, 4, Studi e testi, 40 (Rome 1924) 177-274.

106. Above, 11. For the period during which each appears as a subscriber, see JL, pp. 145-46.

107. Above, 15.

108. JL, pp. 145-46.


4. CONCILIAR ORGANIZATION, III: SCOTLAND, YORK, AND CANTERBURY

1. JL 16836. See also Stones, 29 n. 2. Throughout this chapter general bibliography for Scottish history will be listed sparingly. For the history of Scotland in the second half of the twelfth century, see inter al. Barrow, *Malcolm* and *William*, which include good bibliographies; Stones, xiii ff.; the appropriate sections of Dickinson. The initial volume of the *Edinburgh History of Scotland*, by A. A. M. Duncan, was not available when this chapter was written.

2. See Duggan, "Conquest" 104; Barrow, *William* 10.

3. Barrow, *William* 10.

4. JL 13710.

5. *Fasti Scot.* 291.

6. Barrow, *William* 6.

7. See Dickinson, 137-38; Stones, xxi-xxii.

8. See Dickinson, 138. See also Robert Somerville, "Pope Alexander III and King William I," *Innes Review* 24 (1973) 121-24, where no mention occurs of Dickinson's comments, and where the edition of the long form of JL 12704 in Raine, RS 71:3.83-84, from the York registers, is omitted. Geoffrey W. S. Barrow, "A Scottish Collection at Canterbury," *Scottish Historical Review* 31 (1952) 23-26, provides an appraisal of the position of the Scots in the early twelfth century.

9. See Dickinson, 138.

10. Barrow, *Malcolm* 17.

11. Above, 24–25.

12. St. Andrews was vacant, and thus is eliminated. Moray seems to have been vacant, and Bishop Herbert of Glasgow, who died in 1164, may have been aged and infirm in May 1163, and hardly fit for an arduous journey: see *Fasti Scot*. 291, 214, 145.

13. Above, 26.

14. Above, 25–26.

15. Above, 26.

16. RS 68:1.310.

17. Above, 25–26.

18. For a brief history of the Canterbury-York issue, see Alexander H. Thompson, *York Minster Historical Tracts, 627–1927* (London 1927), the tenth chapter, "The Dispute with Canterbury" (no page numbers); Duggan, 97–99.

19. RS 82:2.744, line 1007 to 746, line 1070, is the pertinent section.

20. See Z. N. Brooke, *The English Church and the Papacy* (Cambridge 1931), passim; Donald Nicholl, *Thurstan, Archbishop of York (1114–1140)* (York 1964) 95–97, although the work of Margarete Dueball, *Der Suprematstreit zwischen den Erzdiözesen Canterbury und York, 1070–1126,* Historische Studien, 184 (Berlin 1929) is neglected.

21. This letter was unknown to JL. It is presented in PUE 2.291, no. 105. For previous papal statements of York's rights the following can be noted: ibid., 231–33, no. 66 (Eugene III); ibid., 149–50, no. 13 (Innocent II); JL 7227 (Honorius II: cf. PUE 2.147–48, no. 12; Nicholl [n. 20 above] 109 n. 102); JL 6831 (Calixtus II). See also Raine, RS 71:2.103–04, 134–35, 138–39, 148 (JL 6553); Anne Heslin, "The Coronation of the Young King in 1170," in *Studies in Church History,* 2, ed G. J. Cuming (London 1965) 175; Morey-Brooke, 154. For general remarks, and bibliography, concerning papal policy toward "primacies" from the late eleventh century and the revival of the notion of *primas* out of the ninth-century Pseudo-Isidorian forgeries, see HCH 3.286–91, 430–31.

22. Stephen of Rouen, RS 82:2.746, line 1063. See also Chapter 2 above, n. 19. The *Draco* offers some historical perspective on the question by noting and commenting on the similar dispute in the late eleventh century between Lanfranc and Thomas of York. Stephen of Rouen (RS 82:2.745–46) even invents a speech which Lanfranc gave when stating his case. See Chapter 2 above, n. 20.

23. Barlow, xli; Foreville, *Église* 277.

24. Above, 8–9.

25. E.g., JL 10742 (cf. PUE 2.105 n. 1); RS 71:3.71. See also Frank Barlow, *The Feudal Kingdom of England, 1042–1216* (London 1969) 297, 300–301.

26. Barlow (n. 25 above), and the references to Heslin and Morey-Brooke in n. 21 above.

27. RS 71:3.71.

28. Herbert of Bosham, RS 67:3.254. See also Foreville, *Église* 277–78.

29. See Knowles, *Colleagues* 12. See also the same author's *Becket* 75.

30. Knowles, *Colleagues* 14.

31. Roger seems to have advanced similar claims against Archbishop Richard at a legatine council in London in 1176: Gervase of Canterbury, RS 73:1.258–59; William of Newburgh, RS 82:1.203–04.

32. See Chapter 1, n. 74, and the discussion at that point in the text. See also Jane E. Sayers, "Papal Privileges for St. Albans Abbey and Its Dependencies," in *The Study of Medieval Records: Essays in Honour of Kathleen Major,* ed. D. A. Bullough and R. L. Storey (Oxford 1971) 65, who cites JL *10324, which was discovered and edited in PUE 3.258–61, no. 118. Note especially 260: ". . . sicut beatus Albanus prothomartyr esse dinoscitur, ita et abbas monasterii ipsius inter abbates Anglie primus omni tempore dignitatis ordine habeatur. . . ." For the name of the abbot of Bury St. Edmunds, see David Knowles, C. N. L. Brooke, and

V. C. M. London, *The Heads of Religious Houses, England and Wales, 940–1216* (Cambridge 1972) 32.

33. ". . . juxta eundem Abbatem Sancti Edmundi, supra omnes alios, resedit": RS 28:4: 1.178. Peter Newcome, *The History of the Ancient and Royal Foundation, Called the Abbey of St. Alban* (London 1795) 72, sensibly placed Robert next to Hugh, but misunderstood Robert's reluctance to appeal. Laurence F. R. Williams, *History of the Abbey of St. Alban* (London 1917) 76, has Robert seated "above all the other abbots of England." Sayers (n. 32 above), loc. cit., speaks similarly, placing Robert in the first seat among the English abbots.

34. See Herbert of Bosham, RS 67:3.253, 255, for Thomas's friendly association with Henry II immediately before and following the council. See also Knowles, *Becket* 78, but note the cautious opinion in Brooke-Morey-Brooke, 191; Morey-Brooke, 99; and the evidence below, 58–60.

35. Above, 13.

36. RS 82:2.746, lines 1059–60.

37. RS 68:1.310. Curiously, the *Draco* (82:2.746, line 1066), uses the same word (*jubet*), to refer to the decisions generally: "He ordered them to settle themselves (*residere*) on opposite sides."

38. See Somerville, *Decreta* 29.

39. This is the frequently cited letter from Alexander to Roger which treats the seating at the council: see above, 25–26. It is noteworthy that Canterbury occupies second place, following Tours, in the table of participants; but can the bias and loyalty of a Chichester scribe be totally discounted here?

40. David Knowles, "Archbishop Thomas Becket, A Character Study," *Proceedings of the British Academy* 35 (1949) 185, also published in *The Historian and Character* (Cambridge 1963) 98–128, and separately (Oxford 1970).

41. RS 82:1.140. See also Reuter, 292 n. 2.

42. RS 71:3.72: ". . . praesentium literarum inscriptione decernimus, ut neutri ex metropol-itanis ecclesiis Anglicis aliquod inde debeat praejudicium provenire, quominus utraque earum jus suum super hoc illaesum omnino valeat in posterum optinere."

43. RS 82:2.746, line 1068. Compare Stephen's language with that of Pope Alexander in the letter to York quoted in n. 42 above:

> Opponit sibimet, ne major quilibet extet,
> Sedibus aequales sunt in honore pares.
> Dum sibi causa gravis voluit supponere neutrum,
> Ne praejudicium quis pateretur ibi.

44. JL 12729. On 30 April 1175, Alexander III already had taken the church of Glasgow under papal protection as *filiam specialem nostram nullo mediante:* JL 12468.

45. Mansi, 22.462. For these lists, see Chapter 3, n. 10.

46. See Chapter 3, n. 54.


## 5. THE CONCILIAR CANONS

1. *Vita Alexandri* 408–10. For an excellent survey of the canons, see Reuter, 547.

2. RS 82:1.136–37.

3. These matters are treated below in detail.

4. Mansi, 21.1182–84 (Edmond Martène and Ursin Durand, *Thesaurus novus anecdotorum,* 4 [Paris 1717] 143–46). Baluze, 2.121–22 (=original edition 7 [Paris 1715] 84–87), and Har-douin, 6:2.2600–02, had edited some of these texts before Martène-Durand. Reuter, 546,

recognized the inauthentic character of these decrees. See also HL 5:2.973 n. 1. Mansi himself once expressed reservations about them, in his editorial note in Baronius, 19.203. For an analysis of the entire problem, see Seckel, "Studien"; Singer, especially 118 nn. 3ff.; Brooke, passim, plus the supplement in Kuttner, "Notes" 536.

5. Baronius, 19.210. For the *Decretales,* see below, 41-42.

6. Binius, 3:2.534. (Binius's 1606 edition was not consulted; the 1636 work reproduces that of 1618: see Quentin, 21-24.) The French work is *Conciliorum omnium generalium et provincialium collectio regia,* 27 (Paris 1644) 368.

7. Labbe-Cossart, 10.1417ff. For the history and interrelation of the early modern conciliar editors, see Quentin, passim. Somerville, *Decreta* 6-17, provides information about the same, relative to the specific historical problem of the Council of Clermont in 1095.

8. Above, 20-21.

9. Holtzmann, "Register" 18ff.

10. Binius, 3:2.534; Mansi, 21.1185. For *Appendix,* see below, 42.

11. For what follows, see J. B. M. Watterich, *Pontificum Romanorum . . . vitae,* 1 (Leipzig 1862) lxxi ff.; Duchesne, LP 2.xxxvii ff.; Fabre-Duchesne, 1.26ff. For the *Liber censuum* generally, see the more recent work by Reinhard Elze, "Der Liber censuum des Cencius (Cod. Vat. Lat. 8486) von 1192 bis 1228," *Bullettino dell' "Archivio paleografico Italiano,"* n.s., 2-3 (Parte I) (1956-57) 251-70.

12. Watterich (n. 11 above), lxxii n. 1. See also Munz, *Boso* 5.

13. Duchesne, LP 2.351.

14. See above, n. 7, for these editors.

15. This conclusion rests on a collation of the text. Niccolò Coleti, *Sacrosancta concilia* (26 vols. Venice 1728-33), has not been seen. See also Quentin, 54-57; Somerville, *Decreta* 15-16.

16. Baronius, 19.209.

17. Above, 5-6.

18. Duggan, *Collections* 20. See ibid., first three chapters, for relevant general comments on what follows. See also, inter al., n. 48 of Chapter 1 above; the relevant sections of Gabriel Le Bras et al., *L'âge classique, 1140-1378: Sources et théorie du droit,* Histoire du droit et des institutions de l'Église en Occident, 7 (Paris 1965); the Introduction in Holtzmann-Kemp.

19. Duggan, *Collections* 22. For an analysis of QCA, see Friedberg, QCA.

20. In its most useful text, edited by Friedberg (see in the Bibliography under Gregory IX).

21. Above, 39-40. For material relating to the Council of Tours in the hands of Antonio Agustín in the sixteenth century, see Laura Gasparri, "Osservazioni sul codice Vallicelliano C.24," *Studi Gregoriani* 9 (1972) 496-97, 510. The portion of n. 108, p. 497, beginning "Al testo . . . ," appears to be a bit confused. The "c(a)p." must stand for page references in Crabbe's edition of *Appendix,* not for an abbreviation of something like *capitulum.* But what the "29," and the "2," following the correct page references to 844 and 907, indicate, is baffling. Furthermore, for "p. 847," 845 probably is meant.

22. Binius, 3:2.534; Mansi, 21.1185.

23. For this collection, see Duggan, *Collections* passim, but especially the general comments plus bibliography on 53. An analysis of the work is in Friedberg, CS 63-84. *Appendix* was edited in the sixteenth century, from a manuscript that has not been traced, by Bartholomew Laurens, and first printed in Crabbe, 820ff. It was reprinted following the presentation for Lateran III in subsequent editions of the Church councils through the work of Mansi. For the edition of Laurens, see Heyer, "Singer, *Beiträge*" 625ff.; Holtzmann, "Register" 18ff. For citations to the printed edition of *Appendix,* the text in Crabbe will be used, with references added for Mansi. Despite the rarity of the former, it is spared the errors which entered the later

printings. For a list of works, Crabbe to Mansi, in which *Appendix* is found, see Augustin Theiner, *Disquisitiones criticae* (Rome 1836) 6 n. 29.

24. For the debate about provenance, see Duggan, *Collections* 53, 136–39.

25. Regarding the two uncontested spuria: in the version of *Appendix* in Binius, at title 2, c. 5 (Binius 3:2.575; Crabbe, 844; Mansi, 22.275), is an item inscribed *Idem in Concilio Turonensi de eadem re*. (In the margin of Mansi is read *Non extat ibi*.) Friedberg, CS 72, identifies this as a portion of JL 14172. After *Appendix*, title 34, c. 2 (Binius 3:2.626; Mansi 22. 391), is a text which seems to be an addition to the collection proper (for the stages of composition of the work, see Duggan, *Collections* 53), inscribed *Idem ex Concilio Turonensi*. This is, in reality, c. 7 of the so-called *Collectio Catalaunensis* of the canons of the synod at Tribur in 895 (see Emil Seckel, "Zu den Akten der Triburer Synode 895," *Neues Archiv* 18 [1893] 397; Seckel, 187), and it occurs in the printing of *Appendix* in Crabbe, 909, thus: *Idem* (for *Item*) *ex concilio Tribunensi* (sic). In two of the three known MSS of *Appendix*—Leipzig, Universitätsbibl. 1242, fol. 103v, and Vienna, Nationalbibl. 2172, fol. 43v—it is inscribed *Item ex concilio Triburensi*. In the MS preserved in the Library of the Dean and Chapter at Lincoln (see Kuttner, *Repertorium* 291; Charles Duggan, "English Canonists and the 'Appendix concilii Lateranensis'," *Traditio* 18 [1962] 461–62, but the later discussion of this MS promised there [n. 20] seems not to have appeared), no. 121, at fol. 42v, the canon is inscribed *Idem ex concilio Remensi*, which probably is a rubricator's guess about his confusing and virtually indecipherable instructions in the margin. Thus at some point between Crabbe and Binius, Laurens's *Tribunensi* became *Turonensi*. See also Friedberg, CS 78, who, *pace* Heyer, "Singer, *Beiträge*" 627, does not follow Mansi and attribute this text to Tours, but cf. *Decretales* 810 (in the notes to 5.18.2).

26. These are at 26.8 and 2.1 respectively. In the edition of *Appendix* the former is headed *Idem*, and the latter has no inscription: Crabbe, 896, 844; Mansi, 22.368, 274. The MSS of *Appendix* concur in the latter situation: Leipzig 1242, fol. 76r; Lincoln 121, fol. 1r; Vienna 2172, fol. 6r. In the former case, however, there is some divergence. The Leipzig MS offers, fol. 99r, no heading; Lincoln, fol. 34v, has *Idem;* but the Vienna MS gives, fol. 37r, *Idem in Turonensi concilio*.

27. Labbe-Cossart, 10.1418–21. For the date of *Comp. II*, see Duggan, *Collections* 23; Stickler, 234.

28. Friedberg consistently calls this c. 2 instead of c. 3: see, e.g., *Decretales* 561; QCA 85; CS 67, 77.

29. See also, for example, the table at the end of Juncker's study of the *Coll. Berolin. I*, 416–17.

30. Duggan, *Collections* 61.

31. Holtzmann, "KE"; this is a revision of an earlier list, published in "Über eine Ausgabe der päpstlichen Dekretalen des 12. Jahrhunderts," *Nachrichten Göttingen* (1945) 15–36. See also Holtzmann-Kemp, xi–xvi. For further information on these collections, see Kuttner, *Repertorium*, and the summaries in Stickler, 217ff.

32. See, e.g., Charles Duggan, "The Trinity Collection of Decretals and the Early Worcester Family," *Traditio* 17 (1961) 508 n. 9; Holtzmann, "Simon."

33. Duggan, *Collections* 60.

34. The Worcester group of collections has not been included. Although classed by Holtzmann as primitive, the structure of the members of this family often is of a mixed variety: see Duggan, *Collections* 95–102. Further, it is in this group especially that infiltration occurs of decrees from other synods into the Tours transmission. Thus the Worcester compilations offer particular difficulties beyond what can be handled here. For a general orientation into these works' treatment of Tours, see the fundamental study by C. N. L. Brooke listed in the

Bibliography, especially the tables in Appendix B showing the appearance of the 1163 decrees in several compilations. From printed analyses, it can be added that the three earliest works in this group—the *Coll. Trinitatis, Wigorniensis,* and *Claustroneoburgensis*—contain no items from Tours: Duggan, as cited above in n. 32; Hans-Eberhard Lohmann, "Die Collectio Wigorniensis," ZRG, Kan. Abt. 22 (1933) 36-187; F. Schönsteiner, "Die Collectio Claustroneoburgensis," *Jahrbuch des Stiftes Klosterneuburg* 2 (1909) 1-154. See also the discussion below, 47, about "c. 10."

35. The qualification regarding the number of consecutive canons eliminates two primitive collections in the French group, the *Coll. Cantabrigensis* and *Victorina I,* and one compilation in the Tortosa group, the *Coll. Eberbacensis.* For these works in general, see Holtzmann, "KE" 58-59; Duggan, *Collections* passim. The compilations are found in the following manuscripts: Cambridge, Trinity College MS R 9.17; Paris, Bibliothèque nat. MS lat. 14938; London, British Library MS Arundel 490. They contain these canons from the assembly at Tours: *Coll. Cantab.:* 2, 1, 5, fol. 87r-v (see Friedberg, CS 14); *Coll. Vict. I:* 2, 1, 5, fol. 240v (there is no printed analysis for this collection); *Coll. Eberbac.:* 2, 1, 7, 5, fols. 211r-v (see Walther Holtzmann, "Collectio Eberbacensis," ZRG, Kan. Abt. 17 [1928] 552). Note also can be made here of c. 2 from Tours, occurring without other texts from the council, in a brief supplemental collection to the *Decretum Gratiani* found in Innsbruck, MS 90, fols. 273-77, at fol. 276v: see Friedrich Maassen, *Beiträge zur Geschichte der juristischen Literargeschichte des Mittelalters,* Sitzungsberichte Vienna, 24 (Vienna 1857) 64. See also Kuttner, *Repertorium* 51, 286; Holtzmann, "KE" 58.

36. See Friedberg, CS 47.

37. For more recent information from Holtzmann himself about this group, see Holtzmann, "Simon." The order of the collections in this category follows the order there.

38. Ibid.; in Holtzmann, "KE" 59, *Florianensis.*

39. This enumeration was available to the author from notes pertaining to conciliar material in English MSS kindly supplied by Professor C. N. L. Brooke, University of London.

40. Labbe-Cossart, 10.1421-23.

41. Crabbe, 907; Mansi, 22.385-87; Friedberg, QCA 90. The MSS of *Appendix* (see n. 25 above) offer the same inscription, but with the final two words reversed: Leipzig, fol. 103r-v; Lincoln, fols. 41v-42r; Vienna, fol. 43r-v. (Professor and Mrs. C. R. Cheney kindly have pointed out to the author that parts of "c. 10" occur in the *Coll. Rotomagensis I* [Paris, Bibliothèque nat. MS lat. 3922A], at 9.8, 15.3, and 24.9, inscribed in each place from Alexander III to the archbishop of York. For this collection see C. R. Cheney, "Decretals of Innocent III in Paris, B.N. MS Lat. 3922A," *Traditio* 11 [1955] 149-50; Holtzmann, "KE" 63.)

42. See above, 42, and below, 48.

43. This and the *Coll. Cheltenhamensis,* which precedes as no. 3, were examined in photostats at the Institute of Medieval Canon Law in Berkeley. Both are classed as members of the Worcester group; see the remarks by Duggan, *Collections* 95-96, 98ff., 104 n. 4. The *Cottoniana* is mutilated at the beginning, but the relevant text can be identified. The relationship between these works awaits a detailed investigation of the developed compilations in the Worcester group.

44. For this collection generally, see Duggan, *Collections* passim. It is a member of the Worcester family: see the preceding note. Brooke, 480, writes "223ff." for 222.

45. Kuttner, "Alanus" 48, 52. See also NCE 1.241; n. 49 below.

46. Friedberg, QCA 90, prints *conc.* in place of *concilium.* See above in the text at n. 41; for Alanus, see von Heckel, 281.

47. Edited by Mansi, in Baluze, 3.382, and repeated in Mansi, 21.1109. See also Heyer, "Singer, *Dekretalensammlung*" 585-86. An examination of a photostat of the MS of this col-

lection gives the same reading as Mansi provided, although there is no gap between the first and second words.

48. Heyer, "Singer, *Dekretalensammlung*" 586, 591.

49. Kuttner, "Alanus" 48, also notes the possibility of *Coll. Luc.* and *Hal.* as sources for *Comp. II.* The rubric for "c. 10" in the first is *De emunatate* (sic) *ecclesie,* and in the second *De emunitate ecclesie et cimiterii et rerum suarum.* Compare *Comp. II*'s *De immunitate ecclesiae et cimiterii,* also in Alanus, with *emunitate:* Friedberg, QCA 90; von Heckel, 280.

50. Holtzmann-Kemp, xv. For what follows, see Singer, passim.

51. Singer, 83–84.

52. Holtzmann-Kemp, xv; Holtzmann, "Tanner" 93–94. For the *Brugensis,* a Bamberg-family compilation, see the work cited in n. 59 below.

53. See Kuttner, "Notes" 536.

54. Brooke, 475.

55. Kuttner, "Alanus" 52–53.

56. Brooke, 475. See also Holtzmann, "Tanner" 93–94.

57. Duggan, *Collections* 49–51, 95ff.

58. Holtzmann-Kemp, xiii.

59. Walter Deeters, *Die Bambergensisgruppe der Dekretalensammlungen des 12. Jhdts.* (Diss. Bonn 1956), especially 324ff.

60. See Duggan, *Collections* 103ff.

61. See the references at the end of n. 34 above.

62. Brooke, 480.

63. Above, n. 25.

64. Brooke, passim.

65. Duggan, *Collections* 137.

66. Mansi, 21.1175–76. For what follows, see ibid., 1176–81. Footnote references will not be used each time this section is recalled.

67. Labbe-Cossart, 10.1418–23.

68. Above, 40.

69. Above, 39.

70. Above, 46.

71. See NCE 10.1064–65, plus the bibliography therein, whence what follows was taken.

72. For Passionei's library, see also *Speculum* 47 (1972) 262 n. 9.

73. See Elio Sgreccia, "Il fondo 'Card. Passionei' della Biblioteca civica di Fossombrone," *Studia Picena* 31 (1963) 122–66; Giovanni Mercati, "Sulla fine della Biblioteca e delle carte del Cardinale Passionei," in his *Note per la storia di alcune biblioteche Romane nei secoli XVI–XIX,* Studi e testi, 164 (Vatican City 1952) 89–113. A perusal of Enrico Narducci, *Catalogus codicum manuscriptorum, praeter Graecos et orientales, in Bibliotheca Angelica* (Rome 1893), yielded no obvious candidates.

74. Bernard de Montfaucon, *Bibliotheca bibliothecarum manuscriptorum nova,* 2 (Paris 1739) 1249, recorded the *Capitula Concil. Turonensis sub Alexandro III.,* in a canon law MS, which he numbered 12, at the library of the monastery of St.-Martin in Séez. Efforts to trace this book have yielded no results.

75. See Friedberg, QCA 85 n. 1, to title 17.

76. For important variants, see ibid., 91 nn. 77 and 94. See also the version printed in Mansi, 21.1179–81.

77. For Piacenza, see Somerville, *Decreta* 7 n. 17, and passim.

78. Francis J. Gossman, *Pope Urban II and Canon Law,* Catholic University of America, Canon Law Studies, 403 (Washington, D.C. 1960) 105–07.

79. See Chapter 1, n. 43.

80. See HE 8.265; HCH 3.388.

81. Benson, 23.

82. *Vita Alexandri* 408.

83. MGH SS 6.410.

84. For the council at Montpellier, see above, 7; below, 54-55.

85. Friedberg, QCA 90; Mansi, 21.1179.

86. This is printed by Friedberg, QCA 157-58.

87. For what follows, see Somerville, *Decreta* passim, especially 131.

88. Von Giesebrecht, 375.

89. COD 174-75 (to the list of references at 175 n. 1, c. 2 from the Council of Pisa, 1135, should be added: Somerville, "Pisa" 106-07).

90. JL 9667. See also Friedberg, CS 142. For this discussion generally, see Terence P. McLaughlin, C.S.B., "The Teachings of the Canonists on Usury," *Mediaeval Studies* 1 (1939) 114, 134.

91. E. A. T. Laspeyres, ed., *Bernardi Papiensis Faventini episcopi summa decretalium* (Regensburg 1860 [1861]) 235. For the date of Bernard's commentary, see Kuttner, *Repertorium* 389. See also the less explicit but similar ideas expressed by Alexander III in JL 13979 *(Comp. I*, 5.15.10; X, 5.19.8), which Bernard also cites.

92. Laspeyres (n. 91 above), loc. cit.

93. Munz, *Boso* 16. This decree has been termed "the first medieval legislation of a universal character regarding heretics" (HE 9:2.347). See also HCH 4.102. For a selection of other twelfth-century texts on the matter, see the seventh title of the fifth book of the *Decretales* of Gregory IX. Arno Borst, *Die Katharer*, MGH Schriften, 12 (Stuttgart 1953) 249 n. 5, citing c. 4 from the synod at Tours, according to Mansi, 21.1177, mistakenly calls it the first use of the expression *haeretici Albigenses*. This term does not occur in the decree. Borst is referring to the *capitulum*, which is an early modern editorial addition, seemingly appearing first in the *Conciliorum omnium generalium et provincialium collectio regia*, 27 (Paris 1644) 363. Perhaps it is this decree that is being recalled in the *Chronicon Angliae Petriburgense*, ed. J. A. Giles, Publications of the Caxton Society, 2 (London 1845) 98, when it is recorded that the Council of Tours legislated against heretics *in Aragonia et Navarria*. See also Reuter, 290 n. 2, who relates this statement to the schism in the church at Pamplona (below, 59), which seems an improbable connection.

94. Above, 42.

95. Above, 51.

96. Mansi, 22.667-72.

97. Ibid., 668, 670.

98. COD 199-201.

99. Lateran III, c. 24: ibid., 199, line 13.

100. *Vita Alexandri* 404. See also Jean Rousset de Pina, "L'Entrevue du Pape Alexandre III et d'un prince sarrasin à Montpellier le 11 avril 1162," in *Études médiévales offerts à M. le Doyen Augustin Fliche de l'Institut*, Publications de la Faculté des lettres de l'Université de Montpellier, 4 (Montpellier 1952) 161-85.


# 6. THE CONCILIAR ACTS

1. *Vita Alexandri* 409: "In the vicinity of Toulouse, a damnable heresy arose a while ago which . . . spreading to neighboring regions, now infects large numbers in Gascony and other provinces." For another example, see Somerville, "Pisa" 112-14; Girgensohn, 1085-90.

2. *La Chronique de Morigny (1095–1152),* ed. Léon Mirot, Collection de textes pour servir à l'étude et à l'enseignement de l'histoire, 41 (Paris 1912) 70–71 (also in Mansi, 21.534).

3. For conciliar *acta,* see Somerville, "Council-Society" 82ff.

4. Hesso's *Relatio* concerning Calixtus II's Council of Reims in 1119 relates a heated discussion of the investiture prohibition: MGH SS 12.426–28. See also Häring, "Notes" 45, following John of Salisbury, for a "rejected" canon at Reims in 1148.

5. Somerville, *Decreta* 26–27.

6. Above, 6.

7. For a selection of such matters at Clermont in 1095—a council with better documentation in this regard than the assembly at Tours—see Somerville, "Council-Society" 84ff.

8. See William E. Lunt, *Papal Revenues in the Middle Ages,* 1, Columbia University, Records of Civilization, 19:1 (New York 1924) 125–26; Karl Jordan, "Zur päpstlichen Finanzgeschichte im 11. und 12. Jahrhundert," *Quellen und Forschungen aus Italienischen Archiven und Bibliotheken* 25 (1933–34) 61–104.

9. Above, 13.

10. See the entries in JL. GP is far from complete.

11. For examples of dissatisfied litigants at Clermont in 1095, see Somerville, "Council-Society" 83.

12. See Chapter 3 above, n. 95.

13. Above, 29–30.

14. See Somerville, "Council-Society" 83.

15. Above, 41.

16. RS 67:3.255. See also the *Thómas Saga Erkibyskups,* RS 65:1.122; PUE 2.298–99, no. 110; Michael Richter, *Canterbury Professions,* Canterbury and York Society, 67 (Torquay 1973) lxxxv–lxxxvi.

17. JL 11664. See also Morey-Brooke, 148: the *MB Epp.* 67 cited there in n. 2 is JL 11664.

18. See the similar language in JL 10905, written to John of Toledo on July 11, from Déols. In this case too, it is impossible to draw conclusions about whether or not the petition for renewal of Toledo's privilege was made in the synod. See also JL 10888, and 10890.

19. See Theodor Gottlob, *Der kirchliche Amtseid der Bischöfe,* Kanonistische Studien und Texte, 9 (Bonn 1936) 143–44. There appears to be little attention given in modern studies to the oath obligations of transferred bishops.

20. This tradition seems uninvestigated. The matter is not treated in Jean-Pierre Pozzi, *Le fondement historique et juridique de la translation des évêques depuis les premiers documents de droit canonique au Décret de Gratien* (unpublished dissertation, Université de Paris, Faculté de Droit, 1953). It might seem odd that Thomas did not know that tradition. Perhaps he did. Is it possible that the shrewd ex-chancellor was seeking to bargain with Alexander III whatever influence he might have in order to gain an ecclesiastical favor? If so, he was prepared to suffer disappointment gracefully, for JL 11664 applauded Thomas's adherence to the papal stance, and explained that Gilbert's action in no sense reduced Canterbury's rights.

21. Hugh of Poitiers, PL 194.1636. (The edition in MGH SS 26 contains only excerpts).

22. Ralph of Diceto, RS 68:1.311.

23. See the following item, and PUE 2.298–99, no. 110, for similar instances of the use of papal letters at this time.

24. JL 10871. See also Hugh of Poitiers, PL 194.1636.

25. Alexandre Bruel, *Recueil des chartes de l'abbaye de Cluny,* 5 (Paris 1894) 558–60 (also in Baluze, 2.122–23). See also Cottineau, 2.1970; HL 5:2.973, where no documentation is cited.

26. JL 10886; Southern, 338. See also Smalley, 107.

27. Smalley, 79.

28. See Chapter 1 above, n. 12. See also Scholz, 57.

29. A. H. Bredero, *Études sur la "Vita prima" de Saint Bernard* (Rome 1960) 157, could be confusing, for Anselm was not canonized at Tours. (The reference in n. 6 should be to A. L. not R. L. Poole.) Roger of York probably opposed Anselm's canonization, for it would have glorified Canterbury, and thus, even if not directly, detracted from the prestige of York. Roger's stance on the issue must have constituted another pressure on Alexander.

30. See Chapter 4 above, n. 34.

31. Above, 25–26.

32. JL 10886.

33. JL 12329; 12330.

34. E. W. Kemp, *Canonization and Authority in the Western Church* (London 1948) 83, writes that another of the petitions at the synod in Tours probably was for the eventually canonized Iñigo, one of the early abbots of the Benedictine monastery of S. Salvador at Oña, in the diocese of Burgos.

35. See Scholz, 57.

36. Southern, 339.

37. See Häring, "John" passim.

38. Ibid., 253.

39. Karl Rahner and Herbert Vorgrimler, *Theological Dictionary* (New York 1965) 71.

40. Adolf von Harnack, *History of Dogma,* 4 (New York 1961) 163 (trans. by Neil Buchanan of 3rd German edition).

41. For this controversy generally, and the synopsis of it which follows, see Josef Bach, *Die Dogmengeschichte des Mittelalters vom Christologischen Standpunkte,* 2 (Vienna 1875) 727ff; DTC 8.756–59; de Ghellinck, 250ff.; Luscombe, 251ff.

42. Häring, "John" 257.

43. Luscombe, 273.

44. It is uncertain whether or not Roland actually studied in northern France under Peter Abelard: Luscombe, 16. The question of the identity of *Rolandus* has been examined by John Noonan in *Law, Church, and Society: Essays in Honor of Stephan Kuttner* (Philadelphia 1977) 21–48.

45. Smalley, 138.

46. Ambrosius M. Gietl, O.P., *Die Sentenzen Rolands nachmals Papstes Alexander III* (Freiburg 1891) 175–77: ". . . dicimus, Christum terciam personam esse in Trinitate, sed secundum quod Deus, non secundum quod homo, presertim cum secundum quod homo non sit persona . . . nec aliquid. . . ." The rubric for the discussion in this portion of the *Sententie* is: *Queritur, si Christus sit III^{a} persona in Trinitate* (ibid., 174).

47. De Ghellinck, 252. See also Luscombe, 252–53.

48. Eleanor Rathbone, "John of Cornwall, A Brief Biography," *Recherches de théologie ancienne et médiévale* 17 (1950) 49; but note DTC 8.757.

49. Nicholas M. Häring, "The So-called *Apologia de Verbo Incarnato,"* *Franciscan Studies* 16 (1956) 108.

50. P. Glorieux, "Le 'contra quatuor labyrinthos Franciae' de Gauthier de Saint-Victor, édition critique," *Archives d'histoire doctrinale et littéraire du moyen-âge* 19 (1952) 225. See also DTC 8.758.

51. JL 11809. See also JL 11806; 12785; Classen, 288.

52. De Ghellinck, 253.

53. *Vita Alexandri* 397.

54. Munz, *Boso* 15.

55. Luscombe, 253.

56. HL 5:2.976.

57. De Ghellinck, 258.

## 7. THE COUNCIL OF TOURS AND THE SCHISM

1. HCH 4.68; Foreville, *Église* 116.
2. Above, 58.
3. See Reuter, 547.
4. Geoffrey Barraclough, *The Origins of Modern Germany* (New York 1963) 186. See also Munz, FB 235 n. 3.
5. MGH SS 6.409.
6. LTK 8.979.
7. See Chapter 3 above, n. 26.
8. LTK 6.475; DHGE 13.507-08. The punctuation of this passage in MGH SS 6.409 is misleading, for the word *electum* should go with Conrad, not Rainald. For Conrad as *electus* at this time, see J. F. Böhmer and Cornelius Will, *Regesta archiepiscoporum Maguntinensium*, 2 (Innsbruck 1886) 4-7; Hauck, 950. Hauck, 271 n. 4, thought this designation of Conrad to be a mistake for Archbishop Hillin of Trier. Victor did convene a synod at Trier in November 1162 (post JL 14476), but Hillin was not *electus* in 1163. Both Conrad and Hillin later joined the Alexandrians (Jordan, 104-05 [see also HE 9:2.77; HCH 4.60; Munz, FB 235 n. 3]). Hauck's portrait of Conrad as a reluctant Victorine prior to 1164 needs reexamination. (There has been no opportunity to consult Siglinde Oehring, *Erzbischof Konrad I. von Mainz im Spiegel seiner Urkunden und Briefe (1161–1200)* [Mschr. Diss. Marburg/L. 1971], a reference taken from Wilfried Schöntag, *Untersuchungen zur Geschichte des Erzbistums Mainz unter den Erzbischöfen Arnold und Christian I. [1153–1183]*, Quellen und Forschungen zur hessischen Geschichte, 22 [Darmstadt and Marburg 1973] 416.) See also Jordan, 83 n. 189.
9. See the general remarks in GP 1.30, no. 96 (JL 10869), and the *Draco Normannicus*. RS 82:2.751, lines 1219-20.
10. E.g., von Giesebrecht, 376; Hauck, 271 n. 4; Jordan, 305; HE 9:2.73; Baldwin, 64; HCH 4.59. Frederick had been excommunicated in 1160, and this action was reiterated at Montpellier: post JL *10626; ante 10708; 10729. Although through early 1164 Alexander entertained the possibility of reconciliation (Ohnsorge, 58-65; HE 9:2.73-74; below in the text), immediately after Tours he wrote that the council had condemned Victor and "his accomplices": GP 1.30, no. 96 (JL 10869). Such language seems to include Frederick, but that view might rely too heavily on later events, disregarding what appears to be a cautious optimism on Alexander's part in June 1163.
11. RS 82:2.751, lines 1221-22.
12. See Ohnsorge, 58ff., for papal-imperial contacts in 1163-64. See also Munz, FB 235. For pre-Tours signs of a desire on Alexander's part to make peace with the emperor, see GP 1.29, no. 93 (JL 10702); 1.30, no. 94 (JL 10758). GP 1.30, no. 96 (JL 10869), was written to the bishops of the province of Salzburg on 29 May 1163, immediately after Tours (see above, 21). It has a curious conclusion, asking these prelates to do what they can toward disrupting an imperial military campaign into Hungary. See also Ohnsorge, 117; Munz, FB 224 n. 1.
13. Mansi, 21.1172-73: "Nos quoque, domini et patres mei, habemus aliquos nobis fideliter assistentes. Habemus enim assistentem nobis gratiam civium supernorum: habemus assistentia nobis merita et orationes vestras: habemus assistentem nobis fidem et devotionem catholicorum regum, qui unitatem catholicam nobiscum et verbo profitentur, et operibus exequuntur: omnes fere, quicumque censentur nomine Christiano. Comparatione vero tantae multitudinis modica est unius exceptio: unus siquidem excipitur, et ipse solus. . . . Sed et ipse per misericordiam Dei convertetur et vivet: quoniam ipse est inter principes terrae multa prudentia et virtute laudabilis, nisi gloriam suam Divinae gloriae praeponere decrevisset. Utinam humilietur sub potenti manu Dei, et principatum ecclesiae suo praeesse principatui recognoscat: utinam intelligat, quia si Christum sponsum scilicet ecclesiae Dominum confitetur, necesse habet et ecclesiam, quae sponsa est, nihilo minus dominam confiteri."

14. The force of this transitional phrase is very difficult to retain in translation. Arnulf is going to draw a contrast between the "catholic" kings and Frederick, who obviously is not "catholic," but considers himself to be Christian.

15. Ohnsorge, 60–61; HE 9:2.75ff. Karl Hampe, *Germany under the Salian and Hohenstaufen Emperors* (Towata, N.J. 1973) 181 (trans. by R. F. Bennett of the 11th edition of *Deutsche Kaisergeschichte in der Zeit der Salier und Staufer*). See also Munz, FB 236–37, for possible reluctance on the part of Frederick about accepting Paschal.

16. Hampe (n. 15 above), loc. cit. For fears of the Victorine clergy about reconciliation, see *Vita Alexandri* 410.

17. Mansi, 21.1173: "Praeterea specialem causam habet, qua sanctam Romanam ecclesiam dominam recognoscere debet: alioquin manifestissime poterit reus ingratitudinis apparere. Si enim ad veteres recurramus historias, certum erit, praedecessores ejus imperium non de alio jure, quam de sola sanctae Romanae ecclesiae gratia percepisse. Nihil igitur plus juris vendicare principes possunt, quam quod in eos contulit dignatio largientis."

18. Above, 51.

19. Munz, *Boso* 2.

20. Above, 21.

21. Norman Zacour, *An Introduction to Medieval Institutions* (Toronto 1969) 195.

22. GP 1.30, no. 96 (JL 10869).

23. For possible tension between Frederick and Rainald in 1163–64 over relations with Alexander, see Munz, FB 235ff.

# Index

# Index of Manuscripts

# Index of Papal Letters
# and Canonical Citations